AMERICAN NATURE GUIDES

MAMMALS

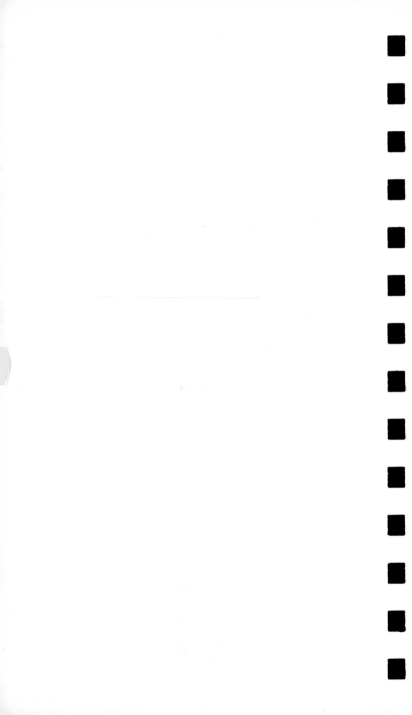

AMERICAN NATURE GUIDES
MAMMALS

JOHN A. BURTON

Illustrated by
JIM CHANNELL

This edition first published in 1991 by SMITHMARK
Publishers Inc., 112 Madison Avenue, New York 10016.

© Copyright: 1991 Dragon's World Ltd
© Copyright: 1991 Text John A. Burton
© Copyright: 1991 Illustrations: Jim Channell of Bernard
  Thornton Artists, London

Published in England by Dragon's World Ltd,
Limpsfield and London

Editor Diana Steedman
Designer David Hunter
Series Design Dave Allen
Editorial Director Pippa Rubinstein

SMITHMARK Books are available for bulk purchase for sales
promotions and premium use. For details write or telephone
the Manager of Special Sales, SMITHMARK Publishers Inc.,
112 Madison Avenue, New York, New York 10016.
(212) 532-6600.

ISBN 0 8317 6973 4

Printed in Singapore

Contents

Introduction

The purpose of this guide is to help the observer identify as many of North America's mammals as possible in the field. However, because so many of them need careful measurement and examination in the hand, those species which can reasonably be expected to be identified in the field are treated in greater detail than those which are difficult, if not impossible. It is hoped that this nature guide will stimulate an interest in observing wild mammals. In order to develop that interest it will later become necessary to consult more specialized books, dealing with the identification of more obscure mammals in greater detail, or dealing with the mammal fauna of a particular region or state. Some of these are listed on p.186.

Observing Mammals

Although many mammals are familiar and abundant, some species are difficult to observe while others are difficult to identify as well. The problems of observation and identification are very diverse and depend to a large extent on the type of mammal involved. By checking the habitat descriptions, you can be aware of which species to expect to observe. A set of tracks may be a clue to what is about and the imprint illustrations may help you decide which animal is most likely to have made those tracks.

A large number of mammals are nocturnal; however with the aid of a spotlight it is often possible to not only observe them, but also to approach them surprisingly close. Automobiles provide good cover for observing mammals. Some nocturnal species are seen regularly in the headlamps of automobiles – unfortunately these same species are often seen dead by the roadside. The most common nocturnal species include raccoons, skunks, foxes, and opossums. By day, ground squirrels, woodchucks and marmots can often be spotted from an auto, and by both day and night deer can frequently be seen.

The characteristics which need to be observed in order to identify mammals vary widely. Deer and other hoofed mammals can be identified by the shape and size of their horns and antlers. Whales, including dolphins and porpoises, and seals can be particularly difficult since normally only part of the animal is exposed above the water's surface; the coloring of the body, together with shape and size of the fins is diagnostic. The carnivores, such as foxes, martens, skunks, and otters, tend to be rather more readily identified – but are also generally shy and elusive. The rodents are easily the most numerous mammals in North America and although a few species such as beaver are easy to observe and distinctive, the majority are nocturnal, small and sometimes impossible to identify with certainty in the field.

Conserving Mammals
Until comparatively recently mammals were invariably either regarded as pests (such as rats and mice), competitors (such as wolves), hunters' quarry (such as deer and rabbits), sources of furs (such as mink and otters), or sources of other raw materials such as oils (seal and whales). However, beginning with the protection of the few buffalo that survived the nineteenth-century massacres, there has been a steady change in attitudes. At first their protection and conservation was strictly utilitarian: protect deer, elk, bighorns, and antelope in order to hunt them. But together with an increasing appreciation of wilderness for its own sake, wildlife is now generally protected for its own intrinsic value. With protection, mammals, particularly the larger species, often lose some of their fear of man. So much so that they can even become a problem.

Undoubtedly the best place to see most mammals is in the areas where they are protected – nature reserves, wildlife refuges and national parks. Not only does the beginner have a reasonable chance of observing a few mammals, but in most parks and refuges the rangers know what species are likely to be found and there are usually lists available. Anyone with a serious interest in conserving American wildlife should join at least one of the many State and National Organisations dedicated to conservation.

Abbreviations

TL = Total Length
T = Tail length
WT = Weight
WS = Wingspan
FA = Fore-arm
SH = Shoulder height

Where a mammal weighs less than 1oz (30g), only the metric weight is given

---

Virginia Opossum
Didelphis virginiana

Size TL 2-3ft (64.5cm-1m);
T 9–21in (25-53.5cm);
WT up to 14lbs (6.5kg).

2½in
(6 cm)

Identification Nocturnal. Most often seen on highways, or as roadkill. Its dense under-fur is blackish with a white base to the hairs, interspersed with white guard hairs, giving a grizzled appearance. The snout is pointed and head whitish. The tapering, almost naked tail is prehensile. Opossums are normally shy, and if cornered may "play possum," feigning death with eyes closed, tongue lolling, and going limp.
Range Widespread in E USA, as far north as the Canadian border area; introduced into coastal W USA and now widespread west of Rockies.

Habitat Variable, but most abundant in wooded country near water. They prefer woodlands near meadows or arable lands.
Food Omnivorous, often feeding on carrion. Many are killed on highways while feeding on other roadkills.
Breeding Usually 2 litters a year of up to 21 almost embryonic young born into the pouch; as mother has only 11-13 nipples, not all survive.
Conservation Hunted for food occasionally and for fur. Not threatened, but extending range.
Similar Species No likely confusion with any other species.

Shrews

Although superficially similar to mice, shrews are insectivores and all have long pointed snouts. The teeth, in continuous rows, are small and tipped reddish brown. The fur of most species is soft and velvety, and non-directional so that they can move backward and forward in their burrows with ease. All shrews are relatively small, the Pygmy Shrew, weighing just over $\frac{1}{8}$oz (2g) is one of the smallest mammals known. Shrews spend most of their life in burrows and runs, rarely venturing from cover, and consequently are difficult to observe. They are most likely to be found by lifting fallen logs or rocks (which should always be replaced carefully). They are usually active throughout the day and night, alternately feeding and resting, and are often vocal - their high-pitched squeaks can frequently be heard as they scurry in search of their prey. Some species use ultrasonics for echolocation, similar to bats. Most species feed on insects and their grubs, earthworms, mollusks, and other invertebrates, but some take larger prey, including small frogs, baby mice, and fish, and some occasionally eat fungi. Although species such as the Pygmy Shrew and the Short-tailed Shrew are distinctive, the majority of *Sorex* shrews are extremely similar to each other, and many can only be distinguished reliably by examining the teeth. Most have five unicuspid (single crowns or cusps), and it is the relative sizes of these teeth that provide the key identification characters. Shrews are often important items of prey for owls and hawks, and by examining the pellets these birds produce from the undigested remains of their prey, it is possible to establish the presence of shrews and other small mammals in a locality. The skulls are usually perfectly clean, often intact and the teeth can be examined with ease. Such pellets can usually be found near the roosts of owls and other birds of prey.

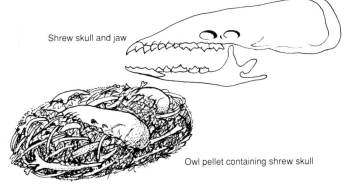

Shrew skull and jaw

Owl pellet containing shrew skull

Long-tailed Shrews
Sorex spp

Size up to 6½in (17cm) inc. tail

Identification Mostly brownish, often paler on the belly. Teeth red-tipped, and tail usually one-third to half total length. Long-tailed shrews are difficult to identify in the field, and can mostly only be identified by careful measurement, and close examination of teeth or skull. Knowledge of distribution can be very helpful.

Range Long-tailed shrews are found over most of North America, except areas covered by permanant snow, extreme deserts, or large areas of open water.

Habitat Found in most habitats from Arctic tundra to deserts, forests, rivers, and swamps. Most abundant in open woodlands, grasslands, and thick vegetation.

Food Mostly small invertebrates, including earthworms, molluscs, insects and their larvae.

Breeding The generation born in fall survives until the following spring, but most of the generation born in spring does not survive the following winter; very few shrews live for more than 18 months. Born naked and helpless, with usually 2-10 young in a litter.

Conservation Several species have little-known or restricted ranges. The Dismal Swamp (SE Virginia and NE Carolina) population (*S. longirostris fisheri*) is endangered.

Masked Shrew

Related Species In addition to the water shrews (p 12), the following long-tailed Shrews occur in North America: the **Masked Shrew** (*S. cinereus*), is one of the most widespread. It has a bi-colored tail and is very small. Mount Lyell (*S. lyelli*) and Preble's Shrew (*S. preblei*) are almost indistinguishable from the Masked and are confined to Tuolumne and Mono Counties, California, and E Oregon respectively. Merriam's Shrew (*S. merriami*) is widespread in arid habitats of W USA, and also has a distinctly bi-colored tail, as does the related Arizona Shrew (*S. arizonae*), which is restricted to mountains in Arizona and New Mexico. Dwarf Shrew (*S. nanus*) is very small (½in (1cm) inc. tail) and has a uniform tail; it is found in coniferous forests in W USA. Southeastern or Bachman's Shrew (*S. longirostris*), is found in damp habitats of E USA. Wandering Shrew (*S. vagrans*) is found in mixed forests in the Rockies; brownish in summer, grayish in winter. Dusky Shrew (*S. monticolus*) has a similar range, but is generally found at higher altitudes. The Ornate Shrew (*S. ornatus*) is only found in California and Mexico, and is very closely related to the Wandering Shrew. Its other close relatives include the Inyo Shrew (*S. tenellus*) from a small area of California and Nevada; the Ashland Shrew (*S. trigonirostris*) from Grizzly Mountain, Oregon; and the Suisun Shrew (*S. sinuosus*) from marshes in Solano County, California. Pacific Shrew (*S. pacificus*) is a relatively large, reddish-brown species (up to 6in (16cm) inc. tail) confined to the redwood and spruce forests of coastal Oregon and California. Trowbridge's Shrew (*S. trowbridgii*) is smaller and grayer, with a wider range on the west coast, as far north as British Columbia. Arctic Shrew (*S. arcticus*) has a unique tri-colored pattern - dark brown on back, paler on the sides, with a grayish belly. It is widespread in Alaska and Canada and around Great Lakes. The Pribilof Shrew (*S. pribilofensis*) is confined to the Pribilof Islands. St Lawrence Island Shrew (*S. jacksoni*) is confined to the Alaskan island of that name. Long-tailed Shrew (*S. dispar*) is rare, found in the Appalachians and other mountainous areas north to Maine; although it has a wide range, it is scarce. Gaspé Shrew (*S. gaspensis*) is very similar and only known from Quebec, Nova Scotia and New Brunswick. Smoky Shrew (*S. fumeus*) is more widespread in NE USA and Canada; it has less hair on its tail, which is also thinner, than the Long-tailed Shrew.

Water Shrew
Sorex palustris

Size TL 5-6½in (13-16.5cm);
T up to 3½in(9cm);
WT 12-17g.

Identification Dark, often blackish above, belly grayish
white. Distinguished from other long-tailed shrews (p 10) by
their large size and by having fringes of hair on the hind feet.
Range Widespread, though not continuously distributed, in
Canada and much of USA. Absent from most of south-east
and the Plains states.
Habitat Marshes, streams, and rivers, usually well wooded.
They swim, entrapping a silvery bubble of air in their fur when
they dive and also run across the surface of water.
Food Invertebrates, particularly earthworms, mayfly nymphs
and other aquatic life.

Breeding Up to 8 young born after a gestation of 3 weeks.
Conservation *S. palustris punctulatus* endangered, possibly
extinct, in Virginia.
Related Species Glacier Bay Water Shrew (*S. alaskanus*),
from Glacier Bay Alaska, is distinguishable by minor skull
characters. Pacific Water Shrew (*S. bendirii*) has a dark belly, is
slightly larger, with fewer hairs on the hind feet. It is confined
to coastal California, north to British Columbia.

Pygmy Shrew
Microsorex hoyi

Size TL 2¾-4½in (7.1-11.4cm);
T 1-1¼in (2.4-3.5cm);
WT 2.2-3.8g.

Identification The smallest mammal in North America weighing around 2.5 g. It is brownish or grayish above, paler below.
Range Alaska, most of Canada, some parts of the northern States of the USA, extending down into Appalachians to SW North Carolina.
Habitat Woods, open meadows, bogs, marshes, sand dunes, and a wide variety of other habitats.
Food Insects and their larvae, other invertebrates, and pine seeds in winter.
Breeding Little known; the litter size is 3-8, but the number of litters is not known. Most appear to be born from the end of July to end of August.
Conservation Apparently rare throughout most of its range, and the Appalachian population may be threatened.
Related Species Population occurring in S Appalachians, is isolated from others and is sometimes treated as a separate species - Appalachian Pygmy Shrew, *M. winnemana*.

Short-tailed Shrew
Blarina brevicauda

Size TL 3½-5½in (9-14.5cm);
T ½-1¼in (1.7-3.5cm);
WT 14-29g.

Identification The largest North American shrew, uniform gray above and below, with a relatively short tail. Its eyes are minute and its ears largely hidden by fur.
Range From SE Canada and NE USA as far south as Nebraska, Missouri and Kentucky, and around the Appalachians south to Alabama and Georgia, with isolated populations in Florida and North Carolina.
Habitat Variable; in woodlands, swamps and bogs, also in cultivated areas, particularly grasslands.
Food Invertebrates, small mammals and subterranean fungi. Its saliva is venomous, and used to paralyze its prey.
Breeding 3-7 naked, blind young are born after a gestation of around 3 weeks in a nest of shredded leaves and grasses, beneath a log. The females may have 3 litters a year.
Conservation One of the most numerous small mammals in North America.
Similar Species Only likely to be confused with the smaller Southern Short-tailed Shrew, *Blarina carolinensis*, which has a more southerly distribution. The Dismal Swamp population, on the North Carolina/Virginia border, is sometimes regarded as a separate species: Swamp Short-tailed Shrew, *B. telmalestes*.

Least Shrew
Cryptotis parva

Size TL 2¾-3½in (6.9-9.2cm);
T ½-¾in (1.2-2.2cm);
WT 4-6.5g.

Identification Grayish brown or brownish above; short-tailed. The only other shrews in North America with short tails are the two species of Short-tailed Shrews, which are much grayer.
Range Widespread in E USA west to South Dakota and Texas.
Habitat Fields, woods and less commonly in marshy areas.
Food Insects up to the size of grasshoppers, beetle larvae, earthworms, spiders.
Breeding Litters occur between January and October (at least in south of range); 3-7 young born blind, naked and helpless.
Conservation No needs identified.
Similar Species Most likely to be confused with Short-tailed Shrews.

Desert Shrew
Notiosorex crawfordi

Size TL 3-3¾in (7.6-9.7cm);
T ¾-1¼in (2.2-3.2cm);
WT 2.9-5g.

Identification A long-nosed shrew, grayish, with a brown
tinge on upperparts, relatively conspicuous ears and a long tail.
Distinguished from all other North American shrews by having
3 unicuspid teeth.
Range Confined to southern part of W USA, and Mexico.
Habitat Deserts and other arid habitats, particularly
sagebrush and prickly pear. Often found in garbage dumps and
also in woodrat nests.
Food Insectivorous.
Breeding Probably throughout the year; up to 6 young per
litter; 2 litters a year. Naked, blind and helpless at birth.
Conservation Abundant; frequently preyed on by owls.
Similar Species Other shrews.

Shrew Mole
Neurotrichus gibbsii

Size TL 4¼-4¾in (11-12.5cm);
T 1¼-1¾in (3.3-4.5cm);
WT 10-13g.

Identification The smallest North American mole, but rather shrew-like, and does not have the feet as exceptionally modified for digging as other moles.
Range Confined to western coastal areas S British Columbia south through Washington and Oregon to central California at altitudes of up to 8202 ft (2500m).
Habitat Mostly in forested areas, including rainforest and redwoods. It is not restricted to deep litter and sandy soils, and is often seen above ground. Somewhat gregarious, occasionally in small groups.

Food Mostly insectivorous; but also salamanders.
Breeding Apparently breeds most of the year, but little is known; 1-4 young.
Conservation Does not appear to be in any danger.
Related Species No close relatives; most likely to be confused with moles, which have shovel-like paws.

Eastern Mole
Scalopus aquaticus

Size TL 3¼-8¾in (8.2-22.7cm);
T ¾-1½in (1.8-3.8cm);
WT 1½-5oz (40-140g).

Identification A typical mole with short, velvety black fur,
eyes covered with skin and feet modified for digging. The fur
is usually blackish, though can be gray, brown or even coppery.
Range Widespread over most of E North America, from
extreme S Canada (Ontario) to S Texas. There are isolated
populations in SW Texas and Mexico.
Habitat Confined to areas with well-drained soils suitable for
digging, in woodlands, meadows, lawns.
Food Invertebrates, particularly earthworms.
Breeding One litter a year; 2-5 young independent in about
one month, mature following year.
Conservation Not threatened.

Related Species Townsend's Mole, *Scapanus townsendii*,
Coast Mole, *S. orarius*, Broad-footed Mole, *S. latimanus.* All 3
Scapanus moles are restricted to western North America, and
their range does not overlap Eastern Mole. Townsend's is the
largest (7½-9¼in (19.5-23.7cm)), the other 2 are less than
7½in (19cm) long. Broad-footed has an hairy tail, the Coast
Mole a nearly naked tail.

Hairy-tailed Mole
Parascalopus breweri

Size TL 5½-6¾in (13.8-17cm);
T ¾-1¼in (2.3-3.6cm);
WT 1½-3oz (40-85g).

Identification The only mole in eastern North America with a short hairy tail. Like other moles it has short, velvety fur which is usually black or dark gray, slightly paler below. As they get older, the snout, tail and limbs sometimes become white. Mole runs, which appear as raised ridges, are seen more often than the animal.
Range Confined to NE USA and SE Canada, at altitudes up to 2953 ft (900m).
Habitat In well-drained soils, woodlands, spreading into adjacent gardens, golf courses.
Food Invertebrates, particularly earthworms.
Breeding One litter a year; 4-5 young; independent at about 1 month; mature in 10 months.
Conservation Not threatened, but often persecuted because of damage to lawns.
Related Species Other moles.

Star-nosed Mole
Condylura cristata

Size TL 6-9¼in (15.2-23.8cm);
T 2-3½in (5.6-9.2cm);
WT 1½-3oz (40-85g).

Identification Easily distinguished from other North
American moles by its 22 tentacle-like projections on its nose
tip. Its eyes are tiny, but visible. Its short, velvety fur is usually
black, and its tail relatively long and hairy; it increases in size
during winter and spring, probably as a food reserve for the
breeding season. Its burrows and mounds of excavated heaps
of dirt are usually more visible than the actual animal.
Range NE USA and SE Canada, with isolated populations
further south to Georgia.

Habitat It is found mostly in damp soils, in woodlands and
often close to water. They are expert swimmers, and they prey
on small fish, as well as earthworms, particularly in winter
when the ground is frozen.
Food Invertebrates, particularly earthworms; also many other
small animals, including fish and crustaceans.
Breeding One litter a year, April-June; 2-7young,
independent in about 3 weeks; mature in 10 months.
Conservation Not threatened - but sometimes persecuted
because of damage to lawns.
Related Species Other moles.

Bats

Bats are among the most numerous and diverse of all mammals, exceeded only by rodents, and are the only mammals that can truly fly. They occur in almost all habitats, but are most common and diverse in the warmer temperate regions and tropics. Although they are mostly small, some tropical species have a wing-span of nearly $6\frac{1}{2}$ft (2m). Most species are insectivorous but some bats feed on nectar and pollen, others on fruit and blossoms, while a few are carnivorous. The vampires of South and Central America live exclusively on blood. Most bats roost in cavities by day - ranging from crevices in rock or bark to caves and hollow trees. Many species have also adapted to man-made structures, including roofs, attics, church towers, cellars, mines and tunnels. Earlier this century large bat houses were constructed in the southern states of the USA to encourage mosquito-eating bats, and also to collect their guano which is a valuable fertilizer. More recently bat-houses, rather similar to those used for hole-nesting birds but with the entrance at the bottom, are being promoted.

Bats are almost impossible to identify in flight with any certainty, but bat-detectors are becoming more widely used, and expertise developed. Bat-detectors transform the ultrasonic calls of bats to sound within the range of human hearing, and as expertise develops it may become easier to identify bats. At close quarters bats can be identified by detailed measurements, particularly the fore-arm, length, shape, and proportions of the ear and the tragus (the lobe at the base of the ear). Fur color can also be important, as can the size of the hind foot, and the calcar (heel bone).

Despite widespread fear of bats, which at times amounts to hysteria, North American bats are harmless, although some species can give a sharp nip when handled. Like nearly all wild mammals, they carry disease, some of which can be transmitted to man, including rabies. However, over most of North America there is no evidence that bats do in fact carry rabies. Disease problems caused by gassing bats living in roofs are likely to be far greater than the risk of the bat-transmitted disease. Any bat found fluttering on the ground should be left well alone; even though it is likely to be suffering from poisoning (from timber-treatment chemicals or agricultural pesticides) there is no point in taking any unnecessary risks. THIS APPLIES TO ALL WILDLIFE. AVOID CONTACT WITH SICK OR INJURED ANIMALS AND ALWAYS WEAR PROTECTIVE CLOTHING.

Ghost-faced Bat
Mormops megaphylla

Size TL up to 3½in (9.3cm); FA 1¾-2¼in (4.6-5.6cm).

Identification Easily distinguished from other North American bats by distinctive leaf-like folds of skin across chin, stretching from ear to ear. Dark brown or reddish-brown fur. Tail relatively short, projecting from tail membrane. Strong fliers.

Range Confined to the extreme S USA in S Arizona and Texas, and Mexico south into N South America. They are very rare in Arizona, and although there are relatively few roosting sites known in Texas some have several thousand individuals. Colonies of 500,000 have been found in Mexico.
Habitat Confined to arid areas, roosting in caves and old mines. Often in hot, humid sites. Often shares roosts with other species of bats.
Food Insects, particularly moths.
Breeding Probably have a single young in late winter.
Conservation Rare, but mostly restricted by available roost sites, particularly undisturbed caves and mine tunnels.
Similar Species None in North America.

California Leaf-nosed Bat
Macrotus californicus

Size TL 3-4¼in (7.7-10.8cm); T 1-1½in(2.5-4.2cm);
FA 1¾ -2¼in (4.4-5.8cm); WT 10-14g.

Identification Has a distinctive flat, leaf-like appendage on
the face and large ears. The fur is light chocolate-brown, with
the tip of each hair noticeably darker than the under-fur. The
tail extends beyond the tail membrane.
Range It is confined to the extreme SW USA (California,
Nevada and Arizona) and Mexico.
Habitat Roosts in groups of up to 100 in derelict mines and
caves in desert areas. They are active all year round and do not
hibernate.

Food Insects, particularly large, heavy-bodied species; they
apparently pick flightless insects off the ground by hovering
and swooping.
Breeding Unlike most other North American bats, mating
and fertilization take place in autumn - there is neither sperm
storage, nor delayed implantation.
Conservation Most likely to be threatened by disturbance of
roosting sites.
Related Species Long-tongued Bat (*Choeronycteris
mexicana*), which has a long snout BUT does not have large ears
is confined to S California, and south to Guatemala.

Sanborn's Long-nosed Bat
Leptonycteris sanborni

Size TL 2¾-3¼in (6.9-8.4cm); FA 2-2¼in (5.1-5.6cm); WS 14¾in (38cm).

Identification The most obvious feature of this rather large bat is its lack of any tail. It has an erect leaf-like projection on the top of its long snout. It is gray or reddish brown above, brownish below.
Range Only known from extreme S Arizona, and adjacent New Mexico, and south to central Mexico. It occurs in the USA only in summer.

Habitat Confined to desert areas roosting in caves, mines and tunnels.
Food Nectar and pollen, particularly from agave, saguarro and organpipe cactus.
Breeding Nursery colonies in caves in USA; the nurseries may contain several thousand females and the young are left hanging in caves.
Conservation Only threats are likely to be disturbance to breeding sites.
Related Species The slightly larger Mexican Long-nosed Bat (*L. nivalis*), which is confined to Big Bend National Park, Texas; it occurs more widely in Mexico.

Little Brown Myotis
Myotis lucifugus

Size TL 3-3½in (7.9-9.3cm); T 1¼-1½in (3.1-4.1cm);
WS 8¾-10½in (22.2-26.9cm); FA 1¼-1½in (3.4-4.1cm);
WT 3.1-14.4g.

Identification One of the commonest bats in North America,
brown above, buff below, with moderately long ears and a
short, rounded tragus.
Range Widespread across North America as far north as
Hudson's Bay and S Alaska, south to S California and Mexico,
but absent or only in scattered populations in most of S and
SE States.

Habitat Nursery colonies mostly in buildings, usually not too
far from water; hibernates in caves, mines and other tunnels.
Food Insectivorous.
Breeding Breeding colonies up to 30,000; usually 300-800;
single offspring, born June-July.
Conservation Despite extensive range, have probably
undergone declines in many areas.
Related Species Keen's Myotis, *M. keenii*, can be
distinguished from Little Brown Bat by its long ears and long
thin tragus; it occurs widely in E USA and SE Canada, and on
west coast of Canada south to Washington. Indiana Myotis,
M. sodalis, occurs from New England to Mid-west USA. It is
best distinguished by differences in the calcar; it hibernates in
huge clusters in relatively few caves, and is very sensitive to
disturbance.

Long-eared Myotis
Myotis evotis

Size TL 3-3¾in (7.5-9.7cm); T 1¼-1¾in (3.6-4.6cm); FA 1¼-1½in (3.5-4.1cm); WS 10¾in (27.5cm); WT 4-8g.

Identification Easily distinguished from all other *Myotis* bats by its huge ears, up to 1 in (2.5cm) long. The ears and wings are usually blackish, the fur long and glossy, golden-brown above, buff below.
Range Widespread but rarely numerous, in W USA and SW Canada.
Habitat Mostly in coniferous forests. Often roost in sheds and cabins.

Food Insectivorous; emerges late feeding 3-6ft (1-2m) off ground.
Breeding Little known; single young born June.
Conservation Little known.
Related Species Southeastern Myotis, *M. austroriparius* is confined to E USA, has shorter ears, and dull-brown, short, woolly fur. In Florida colonies of up to 90,000 have been recorded. Gray Myotis, *M. grisescens*, is distinguished from most other *Myotis* bats by its uniform fur; it occurs mostly west of Appalachians to NW Oklahoma. Cave Myotis, *M. velifer*, is found in Mexico and adjacent states of the USA, where it roosts in very large clusters of up to 20,000.

California Myotis
Myotis californicus

Size TL 2¾-3¼in (7.4-8.5cm); T 1¼-1½in (3.5-4.2cm); FA 1-1½in (2.9-3.6cm); WS 9in (23cm); WT 3-5g.

Identification A small *Myotis* with dark, medium-sized ears and membranes. Has an erratic flight. Foot tiny.
Range Widespread in W North America from W British Columbia south. In north of its range, often the commonest bat.
Habitat In forested areas in the Pacific Northwest, but mostly deserts and semi-arid areas in South-west. Often roosts in man-made structures, particularly in deserts.
Food Hunts low over the ground for insects.
Breeding Single young born between May and July depending on location.

Conservation Little known.
Related Species Small-footed Myotis, *M. leibii*, has a wide, scattered range, occurring in Rockies and from New England south along Appalachians; distinguished from Little Brown Myotis by calcar, and small hind foot; but only distinguished from California Myotis by skull. Yuma Myotis, *M. yumanensis*, distinguished by lack of keel on calcar; widespread in western North America. Fringed Myotis, *M. thysanodes*, distinguished from other *Myotis* bats by fringe of hair on edge of tail membrane; occurs in SW USA. Long-legged Myotis, *M. volans*, is large and has extensive fur on tail and underarm membranes; occurs widely in W North America from Mexico to W Canada.

Silver-haired Bat
Lasionycteris noctivagans

Size TL 3½-4¼in (9.2-10.8cm); T (1¼-1¾in (3.7-4.5cm);
FA 1½-1¾in (3.7-4.4cm); WT 9-15g.

Identification A medium-sized, almost black bat with silver-tipped fur giving a frosted appearance. It emerges relatively early in the evening and has a characteristic slow flight.
Range Widespread over North America from S Canada, south over most of USA. It is migratory, possibly in groups, which sometimes collide with high-rise buildings and radio towers.
Habitat A woodland bat roosting under tree bark, in woodpecker holes. In winter hibernates in similar sites. Occasionally hibernates in caves and mines. It is normally solitary, although some 19th century records suggest it might be colonial.
Food Insectivorous, including moths, flies, and other flying insects.

Breeding Twins are born late June-early July.
Conservation If the earlier reports of large colonies are correct, the species may possibly have undergone dramatic decline associated with destruction of the eastern forests.
Related Species Most likely to be confused with *Lasiurus* spp, which are paler and have more fur on the upper part of the interfemoral membrane.

Eastern Pipistrelle
Pipistrellus subflavus

Size TL 2¾-3¾in (7.4-9.8cm); T 1-1¾in (3-4.6cm);
WS 7¾-10in (20-26cm); FA 1¼-1½in (3.2-3.6cm);
WT 3.5-7.9g.

Identification The smallest bat in its range. The hair is dark
at base, light in the middle and dark at tip. The tragus is
blunter and shorter than other similar-sized bats. It has only a
single premolar. Emerges relatively early from roost. Often
covered with droplets of moisture during hibernation.

Range E North America from extreme SE Canada to Texas.
Migrates in fall to spend winter in caves or mines.
Habitat Very variable; woodland edge, farmland, parkland.
Roosts in trees in summer, only rarely buildings, and caves and
mines in winter.
Food Mostly small insects, spiders.
Breeding Usually twins, born May to July depending on
latitude.
Conservation The most widespread and often most
abundant species within its range; however precise data on
recent population changes is scant.
Related Species The Western Pipistrelle, *P. hesperus*, is
slightly smaller than the Eastern (FA less than 1¼in (3.3cm))
and is paler; confined to W USA, from Washington south to
Mexico.

Big Brown Bat
Eptesicus fuscus

Size TL 4-5in (10.6-12.7cm); T 1½-2in (4.2-5.2cm);
FA 1½-2in (4.2-5.1cm); WS 13in (32.5-35cm);
WT 13-18g.

Identification A large bat with a broad muzzle, rounded ears
and tragus, and fur varying in color from dark to reddish
brown, paler in the west. Has characteristic straight, fast flight
(up to 40 mph recorded).
Range Widespread in North America, occurring from S
Canada and over most of USA, except S Florida and most of
Texas. Some populations migrate to caves in order to
hibernate.
Habitat Normally associated with buildings, including
dwellings, barns, summer-houses, churches; the most
common bat hibernating in buildings.
Food Insects, particularly large beetles.
Breeding Breeds in small groups, or nurseries of up to 300.
In east of range normally 2 young, but from eastern edge of
Rockies westward usually 1.

Conservation Due to its close association with humans, this
species is the one most often accused of being involved with
the transmission of rabies. Due its large size, and ability to
bite, it should not be handled without glove. However the risks
of rabies are greatly exaggerated.
Similar Species Not likely to be confused with other bats.

Red Bat
Lasiurus borealis

Size: TL 3¼-4¾in (8.7-12.6cm); T 1¼-2½in (3.6-6.5cm); WS 11-13in (28-33cm); FA 1½-1¾in (3.6-4.2cm); WT 9.5-17.4g.

Identification A distinctive reddish bat with white patches on the shoulders and frosting on back and belly, the males much brighter than females. It is one of the few small mammals to exhibit obvious sexual dimorphism.
Range Widespread over most of E North America as far north as S Canada, and also isolated populations further west, and in SW. The northernmost populations migrate in winter.
Habitat Mostly in wooded habitats, roosting among foliage, tree holes, behind bark. They rarely enter buildings.
Food Insectivorous.
Breeding 1-4 young occasionally 5, born June in north of range, earlier further south. They are small and poorly developed at birth.

Conservation Likely to be declining due to habitat changes and also mortality due to collisions with cables and towers while migrating.
Related Species The Seminole Bat, *L. seminolus*, is mahogany-brown, with a slight frosting to the fur. It frequently roosts in clumps of Spanish Moss, and occurs from North Carolina south to E Texas.

Hoary Bat
Lasiurus cinereus

Size TL 4-6in (10.2-15.2cm); T 1¾-2½in (4-6.5cm); WS 13-16in (34-41cm); FA 1¾-2¼in (4.2-5.9cm); WT ¾-1¼oz (20-35g).

Identification The largest bat in eastern North America, with distinctive "frosted" fur. Ears short, rounded and blackish. It has conspicuous white wrist markings, and a yellowish orange collar. Browner than Silver-haired Bat, which also has frosted fur.

Range The most widely distributed North American bat, occurring in all US states except Alaska (but including Hawaii), much of S Canada and south to Mexico. Despite its wide range it is rarely abundant.

Habitat Woodlands and forests where it roosts among foliage, or in cracks in bark.

Food Mostly relatively large insects such as moths and more rarely bees, wasps, beetles and dragonflies.

Breeding Usually solitary, with the female giving birth to twins (occasionally one) from May-July.

Conservation Little known of status Hawaii populations (the only native land mammal) are threatened.

Related Species Northern Yellow Bat, *L. intermedius*, and Southern Yellow Bat, *L. ega*, are both similar in size to Hoary Bat, and roost among vegetation (including Spanish moss and palm fronds). The Northern is found in eastern coastal States from North Carolina to Texas; the Southern in S California, S Arizona and SW New Mexico.

Evening Bat
Nycticeius humeralis

Size TL 3-4in (7.8-10.5cm); T 1½in (3.5-4.1cm);
WS 10-11in (26-28cm); FA 1¼-1½in (3.3-3.9cm);
WT 5-12g.

Identification A medium-sized bat with no particular
distinctive features. Distinguished from similar-sized *Myotis*
bats by its short, rounded tragus. It has an erratic, low flight.

Range Widespread over the E USA, but absent from the
Allegheny Mountains; only once recorded in Canada.
Habitat In summer they roost in cavities in trees and
buildings. Its winter habitat and range are largely unknown.
Food Often hunts over water, mostly on flying insects.
Breeding Females gather in nursery colonies, usually in a
hollow tree, which may number several hundred. They
normally have 2 young, which are born naked and helpless and
are carried by their mother while small. At first the mothers
nurse only their own young, but later when the young are
deposited in the nurseries, they nurse indiscriminately.
Conservation In the South often one of the most abundant
bats in and around towns.
Similar Species Most similar to Big Brown Bat, which is
noticeably larger.

Spotted Bat
Euderma maculatum

Size TL 4¼-4½in (10.7-11.5cm); T 1¾-2in (4.6-5cm);
FA 1½-2in (4-5.1cm); WT 13-18g.

Identification A very rare but quite unmistakable bat at close
quarters. Black above with 3 large white spots on the back,
and large pinkish ears. It has a bald patch on the throat.

Range It has been found over a wide area, centered
around S California, S Nevada, SW Colorado, Arizona and
New Mexico, and south into central Mexico, but only ever in
small numbers. Isolated specimens have been found as far
north as Montana, Idaho and British Columbia, and west to
Big Bend National Park, Texas.
Habitat Rocky cliffs and arid areas near streams.
Food Flying insects, particularly noctuid moths; also
terrestrial insects.
Breeding Single young born late May-early July.
Conservation A little-known species that appears to be
rather sparsely distributed. By all accounts one of the rarest
bats in the USA. Between the 1890s and 1960s a total of only
15 were encountered.
Similar Species Not likely to be confused with other bats.

Townsend's Big-eared Bat
Plecotus townsendii

Size TL 3½-4¼in (8.9-11cm); T 1¼-2in (3.5-5.4cm);
FA 1½-1¾in (3.9-4.7cm); WT 9-12g.

Identification Most obvious feature is enormous ears - up to
1½in (3.7cm) long. When at rest the ears are folded up, but
when disturbed they unfurl.
Range Occurs widely in West, with scattered and isolated
populations east to West Virginia and Virginia decreasing.
Habitat Mostly woodlands, scrub and forests. They hibernate
in caves, more rarely in buildings.
Food Insects, principally moths. They emerge after dark and
hover around trees picking off moths.

Breeding The females congregate in nursery colonies of up
to 1000, and in June give birth to a single young, which is
naked and helpless at birth. The males are mostly solitary
Conservation Endangered in most eastern parts of range.
Related Species In the East, Rafinesque's Big-eared Bat,
P. rafinesquii, is closely related and similar but has a white
underside. It is rarely found in caves, but often in barns and
other buildings. In the extreme south-west Allen's Big-eared
Bat, *Idionycteris phyllotis*, which has two flaps of skin projecting
forward from the base of the ears, is also found.

Pallid Bat
Antrozous pallidus

Size TL 4¼-5in (10.7-13cm); T 1¼-1¾in (3.5-4.9cm);
FA 1¾-2½in (4.8-6cm); WT 1-1¼oz (28-37g).

Identification Fairly large, rather pale, creamy or yellowish-brown bat with long (up to 1½in (3.5cm), wide ears, crossed by 9 or 11 ridges.
Range Confined to W North America from S British Columbia to Mexico, and east as far as Texas.
Habitat Mostly in arid deserts, roosting in buildings, rock crevices, willow trees, cacti; more rarely caves and mines.
Food They feed on relatively large flying insects which are often taken to a perch to be consumed. They also crawl on the ground and tree-trunks to capture scorpions and other flightless invertebrates .

Breeding Usually 2, occasionally 3 young, born June or July in nursery colonies of 25-125.
Conservation Probably vulnerable to disturbance, particularly in isolated colonies on periphery of its range.
Similar Species All other bats with large ears are darker.

Brazilian Free-tailed Bat or Guano Bat

Tadarida brasiliensis

Size TL 3½-4¼in (9-11cm); T 1¼-1¾in (3.3-4.4cm); FA 1½-1¾ in (3.6-4.6cm); WT 11-14g.

Identification The smallest and most widespread of the free-tailed bats; the tail is not connected to a membrane along its entire length. Dark brown or grayish above. Ears separated at the base. The wings are narrow and the flight fast and straight.
Range Widespread across S USA, and south through Mexico to much of South America.

Big Free–tailed Bat

Habitat Occurs in a wide range of habitats. Roosts in buildings but primarily in caves and mines. Often in huge numbers, looking like a plume of smoke leaving a cave.
Food Insectivorous, feeding mostly on small moths.
Breeding Nursery colonies may number tens of thousands or even millions. The single young is born in June-July, and left in the roost while the mother forages.
Conservation Many populations have declined from millions to thousands, due to disturbance, poisoning from pesticides, and deliberate destruction.
Related Species **Big Free-tailed Bat,** *T. macrotus*, has a wingspan of nearly 18in (44cm), and the ears joined. It occurs widely in W USA, but is not numerous. Pocketed Free-tailed Bat, *T. femorosacca* , also has ears joined. Confined in USA to states bordering Mexico.

Western Mastiff Bat
Eumops perotis

Size TL 5½-7¼in (14-18.5cm); T 1¼-3in (3.5-8cm);
WS 22in (53-57cm); FA 2¾-3¼in (7.2-8.2cm).

Identification The largest North American bat, with huge
(up to 1¾in (4.7cm)) ears. Easily distinguished from other
mastiff bats and free-tails by its large size. They can also be
identified by their large droppings, and extensive yellow urine
stains on the rocks around the roosts. Their sounds are
audible and bats can be heard when at a height of 1000ft
(305m) or more.
Range Confined to SW USA and extends through Mexico
and Central America, south to N Brazil.
Habitat Arid desert areas, roosting in groups of 2 or 3, up to
70 or more in rock crevices and buildings. They forage over a
large area and may be seen 15 miles (24km) from a roost.
Food Mostly small flying insects.
Breeding A single young; naked and helpless born late May-
July.

Conservation Not known to be threatened.
Related Species Underwood's Mastiff Bat, *E. underwoodi*
and Wagner's Mastiff Bat, *E. glaucinus* are both similar, but
smaller. Underwood's is confined to a relatively small area in
Arizona, and Wagner's is found only in Miami and Fort
Lauderdale, Florida, where it even occurs in the city and
suburbs.

Nine-banded Armadillo
Dasypus novemcinctus

2½in (6 cm)

Size TL 2-2½ft (61.5-80cm);
T 9½-14in (24.5-37cm);
WT up to 14lbs (6.3kg).

Identification Quite unmistakable, the only
North American animal with a hard shell into which the
animal often curls on the approach of danger.
Range Originally confined to extreme SE USA (as well as
occurring in Mexico and south to South America), but has
spread extensively in USA, and now ranges north as far as
Georgia.
Habitat A wide variety of mainly fairly open habitats;
particularly well adapted to arable lands, and generally
restricted to areas where it can dig easily.
Food Insects and other invertebrates, and other small animals
such as amphibians, reptiles, nestling birds and eggs.
Breeding Builds nest of dried leaves in burrow. Produces
identical quads developed from a single fertilized egg. They are
well developed at birth, walking within a few hours. Their shell
is soft, only gradually hardening as they grow. One litter a year.
Conservation Not threatened. Locally may cause some
damage in gardens. Frequently seen as a road-kill where they
are abundant.
Related Species None in North America.

Pika
Ochotona princeps

Size TL 7-7¾in (17.8-19.8cm);
T absent; WT 4½oz (130g).

Identification Similar in appearance to a guinea pig, but
with larger furry ears. They are diurnal and extremely vocal.
They are sociable, living in large colonies. Their distinctive
scats have been likened to black, sticky tapioca.
Range Confined to high altitudes from British Columbia
south to California and New Mexico.
Habitat Confined to high altitudes 8000-13,500ft (2400-
4150m) where it lives among rocky screes, and mountain-
sides.

Food Vegetarian feeding on a wide variety of plants. It dries
cut plants to make hay which it stores in haystacks, and later
removes underground to its dens deep among rocks.
Breeding One or 2 litters of 1-6 blind and naked young,
born in summer.
Conservation Not known to be in any danger, and protected
by remoteness of its habitat.
Related Species Collared Pika, *O. collaris* is very similar, but
with a dark gray collar; it is confined to SW Alaska and
adjacent Canada.

Pygmy Rabbit
Sylvilagus idahoensis

Size TL 9¾-11¼in (25-29cm);
T ¾in (2.3cm);
WT 8¼-8½ oz (238-246g).

Identification The smallest rabbit in North America not much larger than a pika. Dark grizzled-gray above, pale buffy-white below with a uniform buff-gray tail. It is the only native North American rabbit to excavate burrows.
Range Confined to Washington, Oregon, Idaho, Montana, Utah, and a small area in California.
Habitat Usually found in dense sagebrush and greasewood; also in sand dunes.
Food Vegetarian; sagebrush.
Breeding About 6 young per litter.
Conservation Not known to be threatened. Rarely hunted because their flesh is often strongly flavored by sage brush.
Similar Species It is only likely to be confused with cottontails, which have white under the tail, and pikas which are smaller and have smaller ears.

Eastern Cottontail
Sylvilagus floridanus

Size TL 12-19in (32-50cm);
T 1½-2½in (3.9-6.5cm);
WT 1½-4lbs (750g-1.8kg).

2½in
(6 cm)

Identification The best known rabbit in eastern
North America. Brownish above, white below. Underside of
tail fluffy and white. Ears long - up to 2½in (6.5cm).
Range Widespread in E North America from S Canada to N
Mexico, and also parts of SW USA. Absent from much of N
New England. Introduced into many areas, including British
Columbia, Oregon, Washington.
Habitat Very adaptable and found in a wide range of habitats
including swampy woods, thickets, farmlands.
Food Wide range of vegetation, including grasses and
herbaceous plants in summer, twigs and shoots in winter.
Breeding Several litters (up to 7) a year of 1-7 young, in a
nest made in a shallow depression, covered with leaves and
grasses and lined with fur. The young are blind and helpless at
birth.
Conservation Not threatened; subject to hunting regulations
with millions shot annually.
Related Species New England Cottontail, *S. transitionalis*, is
similar to the Eastern Cottontail, but has shorter ears with a
blackish patch between them.Once widely distributed in New
England and the Appalachians, but is being displaced by the
Eastern Cottontail.

Nuttall's Cottontail
Sylvilagus nuttallii

Size TL 13-16in (33.8-41cm);
T 1-2¼in (3-5.7cm);
WT 1¼-2lbs (630g-1kg).

Identification A fairly large long-legged rabbit, grayish
brown above, white below with a large, grizzled tail. The short,
rounded, black-tipped ears are furry inside. The feet are
covered with long, thick fur.
Range Widespread in the Rockies from just north of the
US/Canada border to New Mexico.
Habitat Arid woodlands and sagebrush, also montane
uplands. Hides in a "form" in dense vegetation, in burrows or
among rocks.
Food Grasses, sagebrush, juniper and buds and bark of other
woody shrubs. Feeds mostly in morning and evening.
Breeding 3-5 litters a year, of 1-8 young. Born in a fur-lined,
covered nest from spring to late summer.
Conservation Not threatened
Related Species Desert Cottontail, *S. audubonii*, is similar to
Nuttall's but ears only sparsely furred and longer. It is
generally found in more open, grassy habitats, at lower
elevations. The Brush Rabbit, *S. bachmani*, is a small, short-
legged rabbit usually living in or close to dense brush in
extreme west of USA, from NW Oregon to Baja California.

Swamp Rabbit
Sylvilagus aquaticus

Size TL 18-21in (45.2-55.2cm);
T 2¾in (6.7-7.1cm);
WT 3½-6lbs (1.6-2.7kg).

Identification The largest cottontail with rather short, coarse yellow-brown mottled blackish fur above, white below, and a thin-haired slender tail, which is white below. Their presence can often be detected by droppings left on logs
Range From E Texas and Oklahoma to Georgia.
Habitat Swamps, canebrakes, and similar habitats favoring wet ground, frequently swimming, and even hiding submerged with only the nose exposed above water.
Food Terrestrial and aquatic plants, including cane; also crops such as corn.
Breeding Two litters a year of 1-5 young, in a shallow fur-lined nest. They are well developed; fully furred and their eyes open soon after birth.
Conservation Extensively hunted, but not threatened.
Related Species Marsh Rabbit, *S. palustris*, is a comparatively large, dark rabbit, lacking white under the tail. It is confined to swampy habitats in SE USA.

Snowshoe Hare
Lepus americanus

Size TL 14-20in (36.3-52cm);
T 1-2in (2.5-5.5cm);
WT 2¼-5lbs (1-2.3kg).

Identification In summer rusty brown, with a dark brown nose, and nostrils edged white; most of the underside is white, tail is white above, gray below and the large ears are tipped black. In winter it is almost entirely pure white, with black ear-tips. Some populations retain summer coloring throughout the year. It takes its name from its large well-furred feet that leave characteristic prints.

Range Most of Alaska and Canada, and south in USA through Rockies, and also in New England and the Allegheny Mountains.

Habitat Mostly coniferous forests.

Food Willows, alders, and other woody shrubs, clovers, grasses, and a wide variety of other green plants.

Breeding Up to 4 litters a year of 1-9 young. Young are well developed, fully furred with eyes open. A few days after birth, the young are separated and left in different hiding places.

Conservation Not threatened. Their populations are highly cyclical, becoming extremely numerous then crashing.

Similar Species Likely to be confused with Northern and Arctic Hares.

Northern Hare
Lepus timidus

Size TL 22-27in (56.5-69cm);
T 2-4in (5.3-10.4cm);
WT 7-10lbs (3.2-4.5kg).

Identification A large hare that is pure white with black-tipped ears in winter. In summer it is grayish brown or reddish brown above, white below. It has relatively short ears.
Range Confined to Alaska as far west as the Alaska Peninsula. Also occurs in Old World.
Habitat Open tundra and also scrub, thickets.
Food Grasses, willows, alders and shrubs. Largely nocturnal and crepuscular.
Breeding A single litter of 3-8 young.
Conservation Not known to be threatened.
Similar Species Likely to be confused with Snowshoe and Arctic Hares.

Arctic Hare
Lepus arcticus

Size TL 2-2½ft (60-80cm);
T 1½-3¾in (4-10cm);
WT 6-15lbs (2.7-6.8kg).

Identification The largest hare in America. In winter it is white with black ear tips, and in summer grayish brown above, white below, with a white tail. The ears are relatively short and the feet thickly furred.
Range Confined to extreme north of Canada.
Habitat Arctic tundra, north of the tree line.
Food Arctic plants including willows, crowberry, which, for much of the year, it has to dig through snow in order to obtain. They also eat carrion when it is available, and seaweed in coastal areas.
Breeding Usually a single litter of 2-8 leverets, born in a simple nest in a depression among mosses or grass. they are fully furred with their eyes open, and active soon after birth.
Conservation Not threatened. An important item of prey for many Arctic predators, including man.
Similar Species Likely to be confused with Snowshoe and Northern Hares.

White-tailed Jack Rabbit
Lepus townsendii

Size TL 22-25in (56.5-65.5cm);
T 2½-4¼in (6.6-11.2cm);
WT 5½-7½lbs (2.5-3.4kg).

Identification In summer, grayish brown above, whitish below, with long, black-tipped ears. In winter white or pale gray over most its range (except extreme south). Distinguished from similar Black-tailed Jack Rabbit by having white tail.
Range Widespread in the great plains and prairies from Washington and California, eastward to Minnesota, Iowa, and Kansas.
Habitat Open plains, grasslands, pastures, often in arid areas. It is largely nocturnal or crepuscular.
Food Grasses, clovers, crops, twigs, bark shoots.
Breeding One or 2 litters a year of 3-6 (usually 4) young. Born in a form, they are fully furred with their eyes open and actively foraging soon after birth.
Conservation Not threatened; a game animal in many areas, but also a pest of agriculture.

Black-tailed Jack Rabbit
Lepus californicus

2½ in
(6 cm)

Size TL 18-24in (46.5-63cm);
T 2-4¼in (5-11.2cm);
WT 3¼-4½ lbs (1.5-2kg).

Identification A long-legged hare with exceptionally
long ears (up to 5in (13cm)) and a tail blackish on the upper
surface. They thump the hind legs as an alarm signal.
Distinguished from White-tailed Jack Rabbit by black on tail,
which extends up on to rump.
Range Widespread over W North America, from Washington
south to Baja California and South Dakota, south through
Texas to Mexico, at altitudes of up to 12,467ft (3800m) in the
south of its range.
Habitat Found in a wide variety of mostly fairly arid open
habitats, including sagebrush and creosote and desert scrub.
Also pastures and agricultural lands. They are mostly
nocturnal or crepuscular.
Food Grasses, shrubs and other vegetation, largely depending
on local availability.
Breeding Rather variable, depending on latitude, altitude
and other environmental factors. 1-4 litters a year of 1-8
(usually 2-4) young, born in a deep, fur-lined form.
Conservation Not threatened; considered a game animal in
some areas, and a pest of agriculture in others.

White-sided Jack Rabbit
Lepus callotis

Size TL 2-2¼ft (64-70cm);
T 2¾-3¾in (7-10cm);
WT 6½-19¾lbs (3-9kg).

Identification A relatively large hare with distinctive
coloring. It is gray-brown on its back, and white on the belly
AND the sides. None of the other hares within its range have
this coloring. A distinctive feature of the White-sided Jack
Rabbit is they normally occur in pairs.
Range Confined to the extreme S New Mexico in the USA,
but more widespread in Mexico.
Habitat Mostly in short-grass habitats, particularly where the
species of plants associated with good quality range lands are
abundant. They are almost entirely nocturnal.
Food Almost entirely grasses.
Breeding Little known.
Conservation Rare in the USA, with a restricted range, but
not known to be threatened.

Antelope Jack Rabbit
Lepus alleni

Size TL 21-26in (55.3-67cm);
T 1¾-3in (4.8-7.6cm);
WT 6½-9½lbs (3-4.3kg).

Identification A medium-sized hare, grayish brown above, white below, with the white extending to the sides, but not as high as White-sided Jack Rabbit. Its most distinctive feature are the enormous ears, up to 7¾in (20cm) long, with no black on them. The tail is black above. When fleeing they make enormous antelope-like bounds, and flash the white rump.
Range Confined to extreme S USA, in Arizona and New Mexico, and also more widespread in Mexico.
Habitat Open arid habitats, including deserts.
Food Grasses, mesquite, cacti and other plant matter.
Breeding Possibly as many as 7 litters a year, of 1-5 young. The young are well developed with their eyes open, and are often left separately, or in a nest excavated in the ground or in a hollow cactus, lined with fur.
Conservation Limited range, but not known to threatened.

European Hare
Lepus europaeus

Size TL 2-2¼ft (64-70cm);
T 2¾-3¾in (7-10cm);
WT 6½-19¾lbs (3-9kg).

Identification A large brown hare with thick fur, grizzled with black. The ears are moderately long, with black on the tip.
Range A native of the Old World, introduced into several other parts of the world, including North America. It now occurs in NE USA around Great Lakes to Atlantic coast and in adjacent Canada.
Habitat Variable, but mostly woodlands, farmland and mixed habitats.
Food A wide variety of grasses and other plants, and also twigs, bark and woody plants. Can cause considerable damage to agriculture, forestry, orchards.
Breeding 2 or 3 litters a year, usually of 2 or 3 young, which are well furred and active soon after birth.
Conservation An introduced species, locally considered a pest, but also an important quarry species.

European Rabbit
Oryctolagus cuniculus

Size TL 17-23in (45-60cm);
T 2-3¼in (6.6-8.8cm);
WT 3-5lbs (1.4-2.3kg).

Identification The ancestor of the domesticated rabbit, it is larger than most cottontails, but smaller than most hares and jack rabbits. It is grayish, brown above, whitish below, and white under the tail. However coloring can be extremely variable as many are descended from domestic pets. Their extensive burrows (warrens) are characteristic.

Range A native of SW Europe, introduced widely elsewhere including other parts of Europe, Australasia and North America. In USA occurs on Farallon Islands (California), San Juan Islands (Washington), and Meddelm Island (Alaska); and also in Pennsylvania, Indiana, Illinois, New Jersey, Wisconsin, Maryland.

Habitat Variable, but generally open areas of brush and also agricultural lands. Often close to human habitations.

Food Principally grass and other herbage.

Breeding Makes fur-lined nest in burrow; 6 or more litters a year of 4-12 young. The young are born blind and helpless.

Conservation An introduced exotic, with considerable potential to be a pest.

Mountain Beaver
Aplodontia rufa

Size TL 9-18in (23.8-47cm);
T ¾-2in (2-5.5cm);
WT 1-3lbs (500g-1.4kg).

Identification A rabbit-sized, dark brownish-black rodent
with no close relatives. Stocky, with short, rounded ears, short
legs, and no obvious tail. Most likely to be confused with
woodchucks, which are larger with prominent bushy tails, they
whistle and sometimes grate their teeth when disturbed.
Range Confined to extreme W North America from SW
British Columbia and W Washington, south to N California
and a small area in W Nevada.
Habitat Confined to moist forests areas close to streams. The
entrances to their burrows can be up to 18in (45cm) in
diameter, surrounded with a fan-shaped mound of dirt. In
particularly wet areas they build a cover over the entrance to
their burrow with twigs and leaves and fern
fronds, up to nearly 24in (60cm) high.

Food Forbs, bark, twigs, berries and pine needles. They make
hay which is dragged into a central feeding chamber.
Breeding One litter a year of 2-6 (usually 4 or 5) young,
nearly naked and blind at birth.
Conservation Not threatened; can cause damage to conifers
and gardens, by gnawing bark and burrowing.

Chipmunks and Squirrels

The squirrel family is large and diverse and includes the chipmunks, ground squirrels, marmots and prairie dogs. In North America they occupy a wide variety of habitats, and one or more species are to be found in almost every habitat except wetlands. Several species have adapted to extreme aridity, while others are found above the treeline and many others are highly arboreal. Although primarily vegetarian, many also eat significant quantities of animal matter, including eggs and nestlings of birds. Several species are extremely numerous and the prairie dogs once numbered millions. They were important prey for many carnivores and birds of prey, and their destruction has affected the populations of predators - bringing the Black-footed Ferret to the brink of extinction.

  Although in eastern North America the identification of squirrels is relatively straightforward, in the west it is often difficult. The 16 species of western chipmunks (numbers vary depending on classification) are extremely difficult to identify in the field - he only sure way is by examining the baculum (penis bone). Their stripes, which appear so distinctive are often variable and, in practice, the best way of identifying such species is by knowing the range, and consulting more specialized literature. When fleeing, the ground squirrels, which lack striping on their body, hold their tail horizontally; the antelope squirrel holds its tail vertically. Flying squirrels are almost exclusively nocturnal, and often go unnoticed even though they frequently nest in attics. Squirrels are rather vocal, making a variety of chattering noises, and some "whistle."

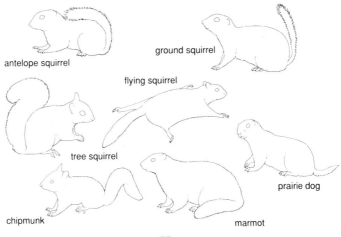

antelope squirrel

ground squirrel

flying squirrel

tree squirrel

prairie dog

chipmunk

marmot

Eastern Chipmunk
Tamias striatus

Size TL 8¾-11¾in (21.5-29.9cm);
T 3-4¼in (7.8- 11.3cm);
WT 2-4¾oz (66-139g).

Identification Rusty red or reddish brown above with 5 dark
brown or blackish stripes, 2 gray or buffy stripes and 2 whitish
stripes, and a bright reddish-brown rump. Its summer coat is
darker than its winter. Their characteristic chattering and
"chuck" call can be heard wherever colonies are present.
Range Confined to E North America north to SE Canada
and south to N Florida, and Louisiana.
Habitat Open woodland, along stone walls and rock piles,
forest clearings, and old farm buildings. Diurnal, colonial and
mostly ground dwelling, though climbs frequently, building
extensive network of tunnels.

Food Wide variety of plant matter, as well as snails, insects,
and small vertebrates. Stores nuts and seeds, carrying them to
underground stores in its cheek pouches.
Breeding Litters of 3-5 young born May-August.
Conservation Not threatened, and usually abundant in
suitable habitat. A major prey item for many predators,
including weasels, foxes, and hawks.
Similar Species The only other chipmunk occurring within
its range is the Least, which is smaller and has two white
stripes each side, which extend onto rump.

Western Chipmunks
Eutamias spp

Size TL 6¼-12½in (16-32cm);
T 2¼-5½in (6-14cm);
WT 1-3¾oz (28-110g).

Identification The 16 species (the number varies depending
on classification) of western chipmunks are generally less gray
than the Eastern, smaller and more slender with proportionally
longer tails. Habits generally similar to Eastern Chipmunk.
During winter months most species hibernate. They are most
easily identified by reference to their distribution.

Range Alpine Chipmunk, *E. (=Tamias) alpinus,* is small and
grayish, confined to the central Sierra Nevada near tree-line,
living in forests and screes. Least Chipmunk, *E. minimus,* is
variable but generally brightly colored. One of the widest
ranging of Western Chipmunks, occurring as far east as Great
Lakes where it overlaps the larger Eastern Chipmunk. **Yellow-
Pine Chipmunk,** *E. amoenus,* is a richly colored, clearly
striped, forest-dwelling species widespread in Rockies from N
British Columbia to N California. Townsend's Chipmunk,
E. townsendii, is large, reddish-brown with brown rather than
black stripes. It occurs from S British Columbia through
Washington to central California and Nevada. Sonoma
Chipmunk, *E. sonomae,* is large, relatively dark, found in
chaparral and clearings in redwood and yellow-pine forests, in
NW California. Meriam's Chipmunk, *E. merriami,* is grayish
with indistinct stripes and long tail (over 80% head and body
length). It is confined to S California and Baja California,
occuring in chaparral and coniferous forests. Cliff Chipmunk,
E. dorsalis, is grayish with an indistinct dark brown stripe down
the middle of the back, and the other stripes very indistinct. It
is confined to Pinon pine-juniper zones in rocky areas of E
Nevada, Utah, NW Colorado, Arizona and New Mexico.
Colorado Chipmunk, *E. quadrivittatus,* is grayish, tinged with
yellow on the head, sides, and rump, it is common in forests
and wooded areas in the mountains of Utah, Colorado, New
Mexico and N Arizona. Red-tailed Chipmunk, *E. ruficaudus,* is
relatively large and brightly colored with tawny-yellow on the
shoulders and sides and an reddish-orange tail. Found in SE
British Columbia, NE Washington, N Idaho and W Montana,
in dense coniferous forests, and often arboreal. Gray-collared
Chipmunk, *E. cinereicollis,* is well-marked with a conspicuous
pale gray collar. Confined to E central Arizona and New

Mexico. The closely related Gray-footed Chipmunk, *E. canipes*, is confined to S central New Mexico. Long-eared Chipmunk, *E. quadrimaculatus* is brightly colored with long ears, accentuated by a white patch behind them, and black stripe below. Confined to a relatively small area of E central California. The Lodgepole Chipmunk, *E. speciosus* is a well-marked chipmunk, confined to E central California, where it inhabits lodgepole pine and red fir. Panamint Chipmunk, *E. panamintinus* is brightly colored with a gray head and rump; confined to Pinon pine-juniper forests in rocky areas of central California and adjacent Nevada. **Uinta Chipmunk,** *E. umbrinus* is very similar to Colorado Chipmunk, but confined to coniferous forests from 7000-11,000ft (2133-3353m) in S Rockies.

Habitat One or other species occurs in almost all drier habitats.

Food Wide range of seeds and other vegetable matter, also insects and small animals. Stored in their burrows.

Breeding One or 2 litters a year of 2-7 young, born naked and helpless in nest in the underground burrow.

Conservation Several species have rather limited ranges.

Related Species Several other populations may prove to be distinct species.

Alpine Chipmunk

Yellow-Pine Chipmunk

Uinta Chipmunk

Woodchuck or Groundhog
Marmota monax

Size TL 16-26in (42-66.5cm);
T 4-6in (10-15.5cm);
WT 4½-12lbs (2.3-5.4kg).

2 in
(5 cm)

Identification A large ground-dwelling squirrel, often seen sunning itself, particularly in the early morning and late afternoon, near the entrance to its large burrow. It is dark brownish, grizzled with grayish, with small ears, short dark legs and a short bushy tail. Over most of its range not likely to be confused with any other species. Gives distinctive whistle when alarmed, and growls and chatters when angered (by dogs and other intruders).

Range Widespread throughout most of E North America from around Hudson's Bay south to N Alabama, and also west across the Rockies to Alaska.
Habitat Woodland, meadows, hillsides, and even backyards and roadsides. They hibernate.
Food Grasses, clover, and other vegetation, also crops. Can do extensive damage in gardens and agricultural areas.
Breeding 4-5 blind and naked young born in a nest in the burrow in April or May.
Conservation Not threatened; considered a minor pest locally in some areas.
Similar Species In west of range, other marmots.

Yellow-bellied Marmot
Marmota flaviventris

Size TL 18-27in (47-70cm);
T 5-8½in (13-22cm);
WT 4½-10lbs (2.3-4.5kg).

Identification Similar in overall shape and appearance to the woodchuck, but yellowish-brown above with a yellowish belly. It has white on the muzzle, and buffy-yellow of the underside extends between the ears and shoulders.
Range Widespread in Rockies from British Columbia and S Alberta south to E California and N New Mexico.
Habitat Rocky hillsides, talus slopes up to 11,155ft (3400m). Makes den among rock-piles or in burrow.
Food Green vegetation, including grasses and lupines.
Breeding Single litter of about 5 young born March-April in nest underground.
Conservation Not threatened; can cause extensive damage to crops, and to backyards.
Similar Species Only likely to be confused with Woodchuck or Hoary Marmot, from which it can be distinguished by coloring.

Hoary Marmot
Marmota caligater

Size TL 2-2½ft (62-82cm);
T 6½-9¾in (17-25cm);
WT 8-20lbs (3.6-9.1kg).

Identification Similar in general apearance to the
Woodchuck, but silvery gray with distinctive black and white
face. Also known as Rockchuck or Mountain Marmot.
Range Widespread in N Rockies from Idaho, Montana and
Washington, north to Alaska
Habitat Usually among rocky talus slopes in mountains
where the large mounds of dirt from its burrows are often an
obvious sign of its presence.
Food Mostly grasses and other green herbage. Hibernates
from October to February, (longer in north).
Breeding Single litter of 4-5 born about 6 weeks after
emergence from hibernation.
Conservation Vancouver Marmot is considered endangered.
Related Species Alaskan Marmot, *M. broweri*, is confined to
the north slope of Alaska; Olympic Marmot, *M. olympus*, to
the Olympic Mountains in Washington; and Vancouver
Marmot, *M. vancouverensis*, to parts of Vancouver Island,
British Columbia. All three are very similar to the Hoary
Marmot and often considered as subspecies.

White-tailed Antelope Squirrel
Ammospermophilus leucurus

Size TL 7½-9¼in (19.4-23.9cm);
T 2-3¼in (5.4-8.7cm);
WT 3-5½oz (85-156g).

Identification Very similar to chipmunks in general
appearance, but paler. Has a characteristic bouncing (almost
"spronking") gait, and carries the tail over the back.
Range Confined to arid areas in the S Rockies from Oregon
and Idaho to Baja California.
Habitat Deserts, crosote bush country, where they excavate
burrows or live among rock crevices, and are one of the few
mammals active during the hotter parts of the day.
Food Seeds of cacti, yucca, palo verde, mesquite and many
other plants; and also insects and other small animals.
Breeding One litter a year of 5-14 young in an underground
nest, lined with feathers, fur and vegetable fibers.
Conservation Nelson's Antelope Squirrel is confined to a
relatively small area of California, but not known to be
threatened.

Related Species Harris's Antelope Squirrel, *A. harrisii*,
which occurs mostly in Arizona and Mexico; it is very similar
but lacks white on underside of tail. Nelson's Antelope
Squirrel, *A. nelsoni*, is confined to a small area in the San
Joaquin Valley, S California, and Texas. Antelope Squirrel,
A. interpres, is confined to New Mexico, Texas, and Mexico.

Richardson's Ground Squirrel
Spermophilus richardsoni (=elegans)

Size TL 9¾-14in (24.8-35.5cm);
T 2½-3¾in (6.5-10 cm);
WT 13-16½oz (369-469g).

Identification Superficially similar to prairie dogs,
Richardson's, and other ground squirrels, have long tails. One
of the most common and most abundant mammals within
range, often seen standing on its hind legs keeping lookout,
giving a loud whistle on the approach of an intruder, as a
warning to other squirrels. Like most other ground squirrels
they excavate burrows. Lives in loose colonies.
Range From S Alberta and Saskatchewan to NE Idaho and
south to NW Colorado and Nevada.

Richardson's Ground Squirrel

Habitat Open shortgrass prairies; also sagebrush.
Food Mostly grass, forbs, roots and other vegetation,
including crops; also insects and carrion; occasionally
cannibalistic. Although they hibernate, they also store seeds
and other food underground.
Breeding Usually one litter a year of 2-11 (usually 6-8)
young.
Conservation Not threatened; causes damage to agriculture
often poisoned.

Related Species Townsend's Ground Squirrel, *S. towns-endii* is smaller than Richardson's, has a wide range in Rockies, from S Washington to SW California, Utah, and Idaho. Washington Ground Squirrel, *S. washingtoni*, confined to a relatively small area in Washington and Idaho. Idaho Ground Squirrel, *S. brunneus*, is only found in a small area of Idaho. Uinta Ground Squirrel, *S. armatus*, is found in sage prairies in Montana, Wyoming, Idaho, and Utah. Belding's Ground Squirrel, *S. beldingi*, is found from E Oregon and SW Idaho to NW Utah and E California. Columbian Ground Squirrel, *S. columbianus*, which spends as much as 8 months of the year asleep, is found in E British Columbia, SW Alberta, south to Idaho and Oregon. Arctic Ground Squirrel, *S. parryii*, is a large ground squirrel, with a wide range over NW Canada and Alaska, where it is the only ground squirrel within range.

Townsend's Ground Squirrel

Thirteen-lined Ground Squirrel
Spermophilus tridecemlineatus

Size TL 6½-11½in (17-29.7cm);
T 2¼-5in (6-13.2cm);
WT 4-9½oz (110-270g).

Identification A brownish ground squirrel with 13 alternating stripes of 7 dark brown and 6 creamy-buff (often broken into spots) on the upperparts.
Range Widespread over much of central North America from S Alberta and S Manitoba to Texas.
Habitat Shortgrass prairies, and also golf courses, pastures, backyards, and roadsides.
Food Omnivorous, consuming more insects than most other ground squirrels; grass, forbs, and a wide range of vegetation.
Breeding One litter a year of 3-13 (usually 8-10) young, born in May, blind, naked and helpless.
Conservation Not threatened.
Related Species Mexican Ground Squirrel, *S. mexicanus*, is confined to the extreme S USA in Texas and New Mexico, and N Mexico; is has 9 rows of spots on the back. Spotted Ground Squirrel, *S. spilosoma*, is found from SW South Dakota to Mexico; its back is covered with indistinct spots. Franklin's Ground Squirrel, *S. franklinii*, is rather dark, with a dark underside; it occurs from E Alberta to N Kansas.

Golden-mantled Ground Squirrel
Spermophilus lateralis

Size TL 9-12in (23-30.8cm);
T 2½-4½in (6.3-11.8cm);
WT 6-9¾oz (170-276g).

Identification Superficially similar to chipmunks with a
tawny to russet-brown or orange head, neck and shoulders;
the back is grayish brown with 2 broad white stripes along the
sides, bordered with narrower black stripes.
Range A wide range in the Rockies, from British Columbia
south to California and New Mexico.
Habitat Forests, particularly conifers, mountain-sides to
above the tree line; nests
deep in burrow, up to
82ft (25m) long.

Food Omnivorous; seeds, nuts, leaves, fungi and insects.
Breeding A single litter of 2-8 (usually 4).
Related Species Rock Squirrel, *S. variegatus*, is largest
ground squirrel in range; found in rocky areas and canyons.
California Ground Squirrel, *S. beecheyi*, is large variable
species, often with pale flecking; common and widespread in
West. Mohave Ground Squirrel, *S. mohavensis*, is unspotted,
pinkish brown above, whitish below; little-known and confined
to Mohave desert. Round-tailed Ground Squirrel, *S. tereti-
caudus*, is similar to Mohave, but its tail is sparsely furred; it is
confined to Mexico and extreme SW USA. Cascade Golden-
Mantled Ground Squirrel, *S. saturatus*, is similar to *S. lateralis*,
but confined to the Cascade Mountains.

Black-tailed Prairie Dog
Cynomys ludovicianus

Size TL 13-16in (35.5-41.5cm);
T 2¾-4½in (7.2-11.5cm);
WT 2-2¾lbs (900g-1.3kg).

Identification A large colonial ground squirrel. Pale-yellowish brown above, whitish below with a short, black-tipped tail. Other prairie dogs have shorter tails lacking black tip.

Range The plains and prairies of Mid-west from Canadian border area to Mexican border area.

Habitat Short-grass prairies. Near the entrance hole to the underground towns, a heap of dirt serves as a lookout point, from which a sentry barks a yapping alarm-call.

Food Principally grasses; occasionally other vegetation and insects. When snows arrive it stays deep underground, but does not hibernate.

Breeding One litter, April-May, of 4-5 young.

Conservation Not endangered, but much reduced in numbers. Massive extermination campaigns have been waged in areas where they compete with cattle and sheep for forage. Towns once occupied several square miles, and numbered millions, but now smaller and mostly only survive in protected areas.

Similar Species White-tailed prairie dogs, all of which lack the black tip to the tail.

White-tailed Prairie Dog
Cynomys leucurus

Size TL 13-14in (34-37cm);
T 1½-2¼in (4-6cm);
WT 1¼-2½oz (600g-1.2kg).

Identification Very similar to Black-tailed Prairie Dog, but with short white-tipped tail and dark patches above and below the eyes. The dirt heap from their excavation are often taller than those of Black-tails, but their towns usually smaller.
Range Confined to Rocky Mountain region of S Montana, Wyoming, Colorado, and Utah.
Habitat In mountain meadows and grasslands.
Food Mostly grasses and other green vegetation. Unlike the Black-tails it appears to hibernate over much of its range.
Breeding Similar to Black-tailed.

Conservation All prairie dogs have decreased considerably, and are mostly confined to National Parks, Refuges and other protected areas. The Utah Prairie dog is endangered.
Related Species There are two other species of white-tailed prairie dogs: Gunnison's Prairie Dog, *C. gunnisoni*, which occurs further south at an area centered on the junction between Utah, Colorado, Arizona, and New Mexico; and the Utah Prairie Dog, *C. parvidens*, which is confined to a small area on the Packer Mountains of Utah.

Gray Squirrel
Sciurus carolinensis

Size TL 17-19in (43-50cm);
T 8¼-9¼in (21-24cm);
WT 14-25oz (400-710g).

Identification A relatively large squirrel, with a long bushy tail. Gray above, whitish below, sometimes with rusty-orange tinge, and with paler and blackish markings on tail.
Range Widespread in E North America from extreme S Canada to E Texas.
Habitat Woodlands, forests, parks, and often in backyards and gardens.
Food Wide range of vegetable and animal matter, but particularly nuts, including acorns, hickory, and beechnuts; also berries, buds, bark, nestling birds, eggs.
Breeding Makes dens in tree holes, or build large leaf nests. 1 or 2 litters of 2-3 young.

Conservation Not threatened; an important game animal hunted for sport and meat in many areas.
Related Species Western Gray Squirrel, *S. griseus*, is very similar in general appearance to the Eastern, but confined to the Pacific States of USA, from Washington south to California and Mexico. Arizona Gray Squirrel, *S. arizonensis*, is confined to three isolated areas in Arizona and New Mexico.

Abert's Squirrel
Sciurus aberti

Size TL 18-23 in (46.3-58.4cm);
T 7¼-10in (18.5- 25.5cm);
WT 1½-2lbs (680-900g).

Identification A large gray squirrel with prominent ear tufts
or "tassels" - hence alternative name of Tassel-eared Squirrel.
Range Colorado Plateau in foothills of Rocky Mountains in
USA, in Arizona, New Mexico, Utah, and Colorado, also
other populations in Mexico.

Habitat More or less restricted to ponderosa pine.
Food Principally pine nuts, bark, shoots and buds of
ponderosa pine; they also eat fungi, carrion, other pines, and
acorns.
Breeding A single litter of 3-4 naked and helpless young
born in a leaf-nest in pines or oaks.
Conservation The Kaibab population is threatened.
Related Species Kaibab Squirrel *(S. a. kaibabensis)* is
sometimes treated as a separate species; it is confined to a
small area adjacent to the Grand Canyon, Colorado.

Fox Squirrel
Sciurus niger

Size TL 17-27in (45.4-69.8cm);
T 8-13in (20-33cm);
WT 1-2¼lbs (500g-1kg).

Identification The largest North American tree squirrel, occurring in color phases that vary locally and regionally. In Florida, often all black; in Maryland, silvery gray with a white underside, in Michigan rusty brown above and orange below; in South Carolina black with white ears and nose.

Range Widespread in E North America, Mexico to N USA, but extinct in most of New England area. Introduced into Pelee Island, Lake Erie, Canada, and many places in W USA.

Habitat Wooded habitats including oak-hickory forests, live oak, mangrove and cypress swamps and mixed woodlands.

Food Nuts, shoots, buds, small animals, and birds' eggs. Acorns, mast and other nuts are stored for use during the winter.

Breeding 2 litters a year of 2-5 young are born in tree cavity, old woodpecker hole, even occasionally a hole in ground. They also build leaf nests.

Conservation The overall range of the Fox Squirrel has decreased in past 150 years; *S. n. cinereus* is considered endangered in Maryland.

Related Species Nayarit Squirrel, *S. nayaritensis*, is similar to Fox, but lacks ear-tufts; it is confined to a small area in Arizona, but is more widespread in N Mexico. The Arizona Gray, *S. arizonensis* also lacks ear-tufts.

Red Squirrel
Tamiasciurus hudsonicus

Size TL 10½-15in (27-38.5cm); T 3½-6in (9.2-15.8cm);
WT 5-8¾oz (140-252g).

Identification A small tree squirrel. Reddish gray above,
white below with reddish-brown tail edged with black; in
winter it has prominent ear-tufts and in summer a dark line
along the sides demarcates the reddish brown above from the
white below. Makes a variety of chattering and trilling calls.
Range Widespread across N North America from Alaska to E
Canada and south along Appalachians and Rockies.
Habitat Wide range of wooded habitats, particularly conifers.
Food Pine nuts and other seeds and nuts; also small animals,
birds' eggs, berries, fungi. Stores food (including fungi, which
it dries first) for use in winter. The remains of gnawed pine
cones, acorns, and other food items, often in piles (up to 6ft
(1.8m) diameter and several ft/m high) indicate its presence.
Breeding Builds nest in old woodpecker holes, cavities, holes
in the ground, or leaf nest in crotch of branch; usually 2 litters
of 3-7 young in early spring and late summer.
Conservation Not threatened and not normally hunted.
Related Species Douglas's Squirrel, *T. douglasii*, is confined
to W North America; it is similar to the Red Squirrel but
grayer above and yellowish
gray below.

Southern Flying Squirrel
Glaucomys volans

Size TL 8-9¾in (21.1-25.3cm);
T 3-4½in (8.1-12cm);
WT 1½-3½oz (45-100g).

Identification A tiny squirrel, with soft, silky fur. Grayish brown above, white below. Its eyes are large, and it has a fold of skin which stretches between the fore and hind feet, on which it glides when leaping from tree to tree.
Range Widespread over most of E USA from E Texas and central Florida north to Minnesota and New England. It also occurs south to Guatemala.
Habitat Forests; roosts and breeds in tree holes, particularly old woodpecker holes; also roosts in attics and bird boxes.

Food More carnivorous and insectivorous than most other squirrels; like other squirrels it hoards food for use in winter. Does not hibernate but may stay in nest during bad weather.
Breeding Usually 2 litters, 1 in early spring, the other mid-summer, 1-6 (usually 2 or 3) blind, naked and helpless young.
Conservation Some populations of *G. sabrinus* are endangered by habitat clearance, and displacement by the more adaptable *G. volans.*
Related Species Northern Flying Squirrel, *G. sabrinus*, is very similar, but larger and a richer brown above. It has a more northerly distribution, and ranges further west to Alaska and south through Rockies to California.

Small Rodents

Small rodents - loosely referred to as rats and mice - include gophers, pocket mice, kangaroo rats, and voles as well as domestic rats and mice. Almost all are relatively small, often nocturnal, living in burrows or dense vegetation which makes them difficult to observe in the field, although some can be seen at night with a spotlight, while others can be found under logs, sheet iron, and rocks. Their presence in an area can often be established by examining the pellets of owls and other birds of prey (see p.9). Accurate identification of many species often relies on examination of the teeth and careful measurement. In the field it is frequently only possible to identify a family, not precise species; known range can be helpful. The main groups of small rodents in North America are as follows:

Pocket Gophers Geomydidae
A group of highly specialized burrowing rodents found only in North America. They have fur-lined cheek pouches and excavate their burrows with their teeth. The species can be identified accurately only by examination of their teeth.

Pocket Mice and Kangaroo Rats Heteromyidae
Like pocket gophers these rodents excavate their burrows with their teeth and carry soil in their fur-lined cheek pouches. They are nocturnal and confined to North America west of the Mississippi, often most abundant in arid areas. They have an erratic bounding gait, and can sometimes be seen in auto headlamps around parking lots and campsites.

New World Rats and Mice Hesperomyinae
Mostly long-tailed. Some, such as harvest mice, build nests among stems, and wood rats build exceptionally large nests. Deer and white-footed mice are among the most abundant woodland mice, and the golden mouse has very attractive fur. Although it is usually easy to identify the main genera, the individual species can be more difficult even at close quarters.

Lemmings and Voles Microtinae
Mostly short-tailed, blunt-headed mice with compact, stocky bodies, often found in open habitats including Arctic tundra. The shape and structure of cheek teeth are usually diagnostic.

Old World Rats and Mice Murinae
These include serious household pests, unfortunately all too familiar. Not native to the New World, but superficially very similar to native New World rats and mice.

Jumping Mice Zapodidae
Much like other small mice, the jumping mice have very long tails and large hind feet; they are attractively colored.

Western Pocket Gophers

Thomomys spp

Size TL 5-10½in (13.2-30cm);
T 2-3¾in (4-9.5cm);
WT 2-9oz (45-54.5g).

Identification Medium-sized rodents with large blunt heads and large incisor teeth and fur-lined cheek pouches. The legs are short and the claws on the front feet long and curved. Eastern Pocket Gophers are distinguished from other species by lacking any grooves down the center of their front teeth. The individual species of Western Pocket Gopher are difficult to identify - most easily distinguished by range.
Range Northern Pocket Gopher, *T. talpoides*, is one of the most widespread, occurring from S Canada south to New Mexico. **Botta's Pocket Gopher,** *T. bottae*, occurs from extreme S Oregon, through California, Nevada and Utah to S Colorado, Arizona, New Mexico and, E Texas, and south to Mexico. Townsend's Pocket Gopher, *T. townsendi*, is a large species restricted to a few isolated populations in California, Oregon, Nevada and Montana. Wyoming Pocket Gopher, *T. clusius*, is confined to a few localities in Wyoming and Idaho Pocket Gopher, *T. idahoensis*, is confined to E Idaho. **Western Pocket Gopher,** *T. mazana*, is found in W Washington, W Oregon to N California. Mountain Pocket Gopher, *T. monticola*, is confined to NE California and a small area of adjacent Nevada. Camas Pocket Gopher, *T. bulbivorus*, confined to a small area of NW Oregon; its names derive from its habit of eating Camas Lily bulbs. Southern Pocket Gopher, *T. umbrinus*, occurs mostly in Central and S America, with its range just extending into Arizona and New Mexico.

Botta's Pocket Gopher

Habitat Found in a variety of habitats including prairies, forests, meadows, and deserts, where they burrow extensively, throwing up characteristic fan-shaped heaps of dirt.

Food Plants, which are bitten off below ground level and dragged into the tunnels; bulbs, roots, including crops.

Breeding One or 2 litters a year of 1-10 young.

Conservation Sometimes considered a pest of agriculture, but probably do more good than harm by keeping soil porous.

Similar Species Other gophers.

Northern Pocket Gopher

Western Pocket Gopher

Eastern Pocket Gophers
Geomys spp

Size TL 7-14in (18.7-35.7cm);
T 2-4¾in (5-12.5cm);
WT 10½-15¾oz (300-450g).

Identification Short-furred rodents, with small eyes and ears, naked tail and long claws on the front feet. Superficially similar to Western Pocket Gophers and the Yellow-faced Pocket Gopher, but the Eastern mostly have two grooves in their front incisors. They are rarely seen above ground and difficult even for an expert to identify. The best way of distinguishing the species is by range. They are absent from the NW States and Canada.

Range Plains Pocket Gopher, *G. bursarius*, occurs from E North Dakota, Wisconsin, and Minnesota, south to Louisiana and Texas. **Desert Pocket Gopher,** *G. arenarius*, occurs in S New Mexico, adjacent Texas and Mexico. Texas Pocket Gopher, *G. personatus*, is confined to extreme S Texas and adjacent Mexico. **Southeastern Pocket Gopher,** *G. pinetis*, is found in N Florida, S Georgia and SE Alabama. Colonial Pocket Gopher, *G. colonus*, is confined to the coast of SE Georgia, Sherman's Pocket Gopher, *G. fontanelus*, to NE Georgia, and the Cumberland Island Pocket Gopher, *G. cumberlandius*, to Cumberland Island, off Georgia.

Southeastern
Pocket Gopher

Habitat A wide variety of habitats generally with loose sandy soils, where they burrow extensively. In snow-bound areas, when the snow melts, cores of dirt from their burrows are left exposed. Unlike most rodents they cannot swim, and

rivers often mark the boundaries of populations or species.
Food Almost entirely vegetable matter, particularly roots
and bulbs. Food is stored in undergound chambers.
Breeding 2-6 (usually 4) young born in spring, blind,
naked, and helpless.

Plains Pocket Gopher

Conservation Several species have rather restricted ranges.
Locally they can be pests of agriculture, but have a relatively
slow reproductive rate compared with most other rodents.
Related Species Yellow-faced Pocket Gopher, *Pappogeomys
castanops*, a yellowish-brown species with dark feet, can be
distinguished from Western and Eastern Pocket Gophers by its
single groove on its incisors. It occurs from SE Colorado, to
Mexico.

Desert Pocket Gopher

Pocket Mice
Perognathus spp

Size TL 4-9in (10-22cm);
T 1¾-5½in (4.5-14.5cm);
WT ¼-1½oz (7-47g).

Identification Pocket mice are small jumping rodents, with a
long tail and relatively long hind limbs, and short forelimbs.
They have fur-lined cheek pouches. Most species are yellowish,
grayish or brown above, and white on the belly, and the long
furry tail is usually dark with a white stripe on both sides, and a
tuft toward the end. The precise identification of pocket mice is
often extremely difficult, even in the laboratory; range and
intensity of coloring and markings are useful, but some species
can only be identified by such minute details as tooth shape and
the shape of the male's penis.

Bailey's Pocket Mouse

Range Olive Backed Pocket Mouse, *P. fasciatus,* from S
Alberta, S Saskatchewan and S Manitoba, south to Colorado
and N Nebraska. Plains Pocket Mouse, *P. flavescens* (inc.
apache), occurs from North Dakota and Minnesota to Texas
and Arizona. Silky Pocket Mouse, *P. flavus*, is found from W
Nebraska south to Mexico. **Little Pocket Mouse,**
P. longimembris, occurs from SE Oregon to Mexico, and west to
Utah, but range highly fragmented. Arizona Pocket Mouse,
P. amplus occurs in a relatively small area from N Mexico to
Arizona. Great Basin Pocket Mouse, *P. parvus*, is found from S
British Columbia to E California and Utah. White-eared
Pocket Mouse, *P. alticola*, and Yellow-eared Pocket Mouse,
P. xanthonotus, are confined to south-central California, and
San Joaquin Pocket Mouse, *P. inornatus*, to San Joaquin Valley,

California. Long-tailed Pocket Mouse, *P. formosus*, is found from Nevada and W Utah to Baja California. **Bailey's Pocket Mouse,** *P. baileyi*, is found around USA/Mexico border in Mexico, California, Arizona, and New Mexico. Hispid Pocket Mouse, *P. hispidus*, has a wide range from southern N Dakota to Mexico. Rock Pocket Mouse, *P. intermedius* and Desert Pocket Mouse, *P. pencillatus*, are both widespread in SW USA and New Mexico. Nelson's Pocket Mouse, *P. nelsoni*, is found in W Texas and S New Mexico south to Mexico. San Diego Pocket Mouse, *P. fallax*, occurs from S California to Baja California, and California Pocket Mouse, *P. californicus*, and Spiny Pocket Mouse, *P. spinatus*, are found from central California to N Baja California.

Habitat Mostly in rather arid habitats, including plains, prairies, and deserts, where they are nocturnal, spending the day in burrows which they excavate themselves. In some species the entrances to their burrows are conspicuous mounds of dirt. Some species plug the entrance holes during the day to maintain a constant temperature and humidity. Some species hibernate or estivate, in burrows up to nearly 6½ft (2m) deep.

Food Mostly seeds, with some green vegetable matter, and occasionally insects. The cheek pouches are used to carry food underground where it is stored. Most species are able to survive without drinking water, by metabolizing water from their food.

Little Pocket Mouse

Breeding Litters usually 1-8, with several litters a year
Conservation Not known to be threatened.
Related Species Mexican Spiny Pocket Mouse, *Liomys irroratus*, which is found in Mexico and also in extreme S Texas. It is distinguished from true pocket mice by its lack of grooves on its teeth.

Dark Kangaroo Mouse
Microdipodops megalocephalus

1in
(2.5 cm)

Size TL 5¾-6¾in (14.8-17.7cm);
T 2½-4in (6.8-10.3cm);
WT 10-17g.

Identification Dark brown or grayish black above, paler below. Separated from kangaroo rats and pocket mice by particularly furry soles to feet; tail wider at the middle and tapering at both ends. Distinguished from the slightly smaller Pale Kangaroo Mouse by proportionally larger hind foot and darker coloration.

Range Widespread, but not continuous, east of the Sierra Nevada in the Great Basin region. It is often very abundant.

Habitat Generally sagebrush deserts, typically gravelly soils. In the colder regions it probably hibernates.

Food Grasses and desert forbs, seeds and insects. They can exist without water, metabolizing it from their food. Like most other desert-dwelling rodents they store food, carrying it underground in the cheek pouches.

Breeding Build an elaborate nest underground, and breed between late March and late September with litters of 2-7 young, which are naked and blind at birth.

Conservation Not threatened; locally abundant

Related Species Pale Kangaroo Mouse, *M. pallidus*, which is confined to W Nevada and a small area of adjacent E California; it is paler above with pure white underparts.

Kangaroo Rats
Dipodomys spp

Size TL 8-14½in (20-37.7cm);
T 4-8¼in (10-21.5cm);
WT 1¼-6¼oz (35-180g).

Identification Like kangaroo mice, but generally larger; they
have long, powerful hind limbs, and rather short fore limbs.
Most species are buff or brownish or grayish above, pale
below, and have long tails tufted at the end. Distinguished
from pocket and kangaroo mice by the tail which has an
obvious white stripe along each side; most species have a white
stripe on the thigh. They are one of the most frequently
observed nocturnal mammals in desert areas, crossing roads,
or visiting campsites. Individual species are often difficult to
identify and best distinguished by distribution, and relative
density of coloration.

Range Confined to W North America, from S Canada to
central Mexico. Ord's Kangaroo Rat, *D. ordii*, is one of the
most widely distributed, occurring from S Alberta and S
Saskatchewan to central Mexico. Chisel-toothed Kangaroo
Rat, *D. microps*, occurs from S Oregon to California, Nevada,
Utah, and N Arizona. Agile Kangaroo Rat, *D. agilis*, is
confined to SW California and Baja California. Heerman's
Kangaroo Rat, *D. heermanni*, has a restricted range in S
California. In California, **Giant Kangaroo Rat,** *D. ingens*, is
confined to W San Joaquin Valley. Big-eared Kangaroo Rat,
D. elephantinus, is confined to San Benito County, and
Narrow-faced Kangaroo Rat, *D. venustus*, is confined to the

Banner-tailed
Kangaroo Rat

Monterey and Santa Cruz areas. Stephen's Kangaroo Rat, *D. stephensi*, is confined to San Jacinto Valley and California Kangaroo Rat, *D. californicus*, is confined to S Oregon and N California. Panamint Kangaroo Rat, *D. panamintinus*, has a rather fragmented range in E and S California, and a small area of W Nevada. **Banner-tailed Kangaroo Rat,** *D. spectabilis*, is found in Arizona, New Mexico, W Texas, and N Mexico; it has a spectacular tail ending in a pure white tuft, preceded by a blackish band. Texas Kangaroo Rat, *D. elator*, is confined to a small area straddling the Texas/Oklahoma border. Rat Kangaroo Rat, *D. deserti*, is found in SW Nevada, SE California, SW Arizona, and NW Mexico. Merriam's Kangaroo Rat, *D. merriami*, is found in N Mexico, and SW USA as far north as NW Nevada. It is the smallest kangaroo rat, closely related to the Fresno Kangaroo Rat, *D. nitratoides*, which is confined to San Joaquin Valley, California.

Habitat Mostly in deserts and other arid areas, excavating burrows, often near the base of creosote bush, mesquite, sage brush.

Food Seeds, forbs, grasses, and some insects. Like most other desert-dwelling rodents they store food underground.

Breeding Nest in chamber in their underground burrows. One or 2 litters a year, possibly a third in some species, of 1-8 young, naked and helpless at birth.

Conservation Several species have restricted ranges, particularly in California. Those listed as threatened or endangered or with very restricted ranges include: *D. stephensi*, *D. elephantinus*, *D. ingens*, *D. nitratoides*.

Similar Species Pocket mice and kangaroo mice.

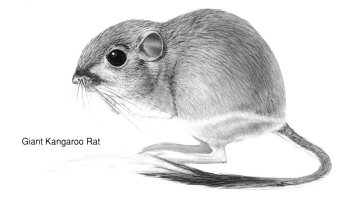

Giant Kangaroo Rat

Beaver
Castor canadensis

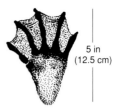

5 in
(12.5 cm)

Size TL 3-4ft (90cm-1.2m);
T 12-17in (30-44cm);
WT 44-60lbs (20-27kg).

Identification A large dark blackish-brown aquatic rodent,
with a broad, flat tail. Only likely to be confused with musk
rats and nutria, both of which have slender tails. When
disturbed slaps tail on surface of water before diving. The
most obvious feature are its large dams, built from twigs and
branches, filled with mud, and lodges up to 6½ft (2m) high
and 39ft (12m) across. Gnawed twigs, branches, and tree
trunks are also characteristic. They can stay submerged for up
to 15 mins.

Range Formerly occurred in almost all wetland habitats,
except those permanently frozen, from Alaska and N Canada
to Mexico, but absent from most of Florida and much of
California and Nevada.

Habitat Rivers, swamps, marshes, lakes, and ponds.

Food Twigs, leaves, and a wide variety of vegetation. In the
fall twigs and branches are taken under water for use in winter.

Breeding One to 8 (usually 4 or 5) young (kits) are born in
the lodge, and are well developed, fully furred, with their eyes
open, and can swim within a week of birth.

Conservation Although exterminated from many areas, it is
now protected and managed in most areas, and spreading its
range, often helped by reintroductions.

Marsh Rice Rat
Oryzomys palustris

Size TL 7¼-12in (18.7-30.5cm);
T 3¼-6in (8.4-15.6cm);
WT 1-2¾oz (30-78g).

Identification A medium-sized rat, grayish brown above,
pale below, with a long, sparsely furred tail and whitish feet.
They are nocturnal and rarely seen, despite being very
abundant. The Brown Rat is larger, with a shorter, thicker tail,
and wood rats are larger, white below and have larger ears.
Range SE USA, from E Texas, north to SE Kansas, S
Kentucky, and along East Coast to S New Jersey.
Habitat Wide range, including salt marshes, woodland
clearings, but generally in areas with grasses or sedges. They
are amphibious, and tunnel extensively. They build nests of
grass and sedge in low bush or rushes, often over water.
Food Omnivorous, but principally grain and seeds, plants as
well as insects and small crabs, depending on habitat. Also
occasionally eggs and young of birds.

Breeding One to 5 young born blind and naked, but develop
rapidly and are active at about 6 days and are weaned at 11.
Conservation Locally a pest.
Related Species Coue's Rice Rat, *O. couesi*, is a Mexican
species which also occurs in the Rio Grande Valley, Mexico;
Key Rice Rat, *O. argentatus*, is confined to Cudjoe Key,
Florida and is considered endangered.

Harvest Mice
Reithrodontomys spp

Size TL 4-7¾in (10.7-20cm);
T 1¾-4½in (4.5-11.6cm);
WT 6-30g.

Identification Similar to House Mouse, but with more fur on tail, and grooves on upper incisors. Generally brownish above, white below; some have dark center to back, and most have large ears.
Range Plains Harvest Mouse, *R. montanus*, is found in prairies from S North Dakota to Texas, Arizona, and Mexico. Eastern Harvest Mouse, *R. humulis*, is widespread in E USA, from SE Texas, north to Virginia, Pennsylvania, and Delaware. **Western Harvest Mouse,** *R. megalotis*, occurs in dry open habitats over much of W USA, and also extreme south W Canada, and into Mexico. Salt-marsh Harvest Mouse, *R. raviventris*, is confined to a small area in San Francisco Bay. Fulvous Harvest Mouse, *R. fulvescens*, is found in SE USA and Mexico.
Habitat They are mostly found in open grassy habitats, where they are agile climbers. They build nests on or above ground level, some from grasses, shredded bark and other fibers in a burrow.
Food Mostly seeds and vegetation, but also insects and other small invertebrates. Some seeds are stored.
Breeding Most breed throughout the year, except in the north. 1-9 young in a litter, helpless at birth.
Conservation Salt-marsh Harvest Mouse is threatened.
Similar Species House Mouse or possibly jumping mice.

Western Harvest Mouse

Golden Mouse
Ochrotomys nuttalli

Size TL 5½-7¼in (14-19cm);
T 2½-3¾in (6.8-9.5cm);
WT 13-27g.

Identification An attractive mouse with thick, soft fur which is tawny brown above, more golden on sides, and creamy white below. Its tail is relatively short, prehensile, and slightly bicolored. The coloring is quite unlike any other rats or mice, except possibly jumping mice, which have much longer tails.
Range From E Texas to central Virginia, and central Florida.
Habitat Found in a wide variety of habitats, including woodlands, boulder-strewn mountain-sides, lowland thickets, and swamps. In some parts of its range it is highly arboreal, building a nest in trees, vines or even Spanish Moss, up to 30ft (9m) off the ground. It is nocturnal and also gregarious with up to eight in a nest, and it does not hibernate.

Food Mostly seeds, but also other vegetable matter and some insects. Loosely constructed feeding platforms are made in vegetation, on which food remains accumulate.
Breeding In the south they probably breed all the year round, in the north from March to October. There are several litters a year of 1-4 (usually 2-3) young born naked and blind.
Conservation Not threatened.
Similar Species Most likely to be confused with deer (*Peromyscus*) mice.

Deer Mice
Peromyscus spp

Size TL 4½-11in (11.9-28.5cm);
T 1½-6in (4-15.6cm);
WT ¼-2oz (8-55g).

¼in
(0.5 cm)

Identification Among the most widespread and often most abundant mice in North America. They are generally dark brown, orange brown, yellowish or grayish above, white below. They have large eyes, prominent ears and long tails. The individual species are often difficult to separate, but range is helpful in deciding on the species encountered.

Range Deer Mouse, *P. maniculatus*, is one of the smallest, and also the most widespread occurring over most of Canada and USA except much of SE USA and W Mexico. **White-footed Mouse,** *P. leucopus*, is very similar to Deer Mouse but has a more easterly distribution; they overlap extensively in the Plains states of USA. Cactus Mouse, *P. eremicus*, is found in desert habitats in SW USA and Mexico. Merriam's Mouse, *P. merri-ami*, is only known from a few areas in S Arizona and Mexico. California Mouse, *P. californicus*, is the largest deer mouse, found in SW and Baja California; also known as the Parasitic Mouse, because it lives in the nests of wood rats. Oldfield Mouse, *P. polionotus*, is confined to N Florida, Georgia, E Alabama and South Carolina. Cotton Mouse, *P. gossypinus*, occurs along coast from SE Virginia to Florida, and in SE USA north to Kentucky. Canyon Mouse, *P. crinitus*, occurs in rocky habitats from Oregon and SW Idaho south to Baja California.

Deer Mouse

Brush Mouse, *P. boylii*, is found in arid habitats over much of S USA from W Arkansas, westward. Texas Mouse, *P. attwateri*, is closely related to Brush Mouse and found in E central Texas, to SW Missouri. White-ankled Mouse, *P. pectoralis*, is found in rocky habitats in Texas and adjacent states. Pinion Mouse, *P. truei*, is associated (but not exclusively) with Pinion pine habitats in W USA from S Oregon to W Oklahoma. The closely related Palo Duro Mouse, *P. comanche*, is confined to W Texas. Rock Mouse, *P. difficilis (=nasutus)*, is found in arid rocky habitats from W Colorado and E Utah south to Mexico. Florida Mouse, *P. floridanus*, is confined to peninsular Florida, where it is usually associated with Gopher Tortoise burrows.

Habitat Deer mice are found in almost all habitats, ranging from wet woodlands to arid deserts.

Food Wide range of nuts, berries, seeds, and other vegetation, and also insects; food is stored.

Breeding Some species breed all the year round, particularly in the warmer areas. Up to 4 or more litters a year, of 1-9 young, which are born naked and blind.

Conservation Some species with isolated populations are threatened, particularly in Florida.

Similar Species Similar to many other species of mice, but most closely related to the Golden Mouse.

White-footed Mouse

Northern Pygmy Mouse
Baiomys taylori

Size TL 3¼-4¾in (8.7-12.3cm);
T 1¼-2in (3.4-5.3cm);
WT 7-10g.

Identification Tiny; one of the smallest mice, not much more than half the size of a House Mouse. Grayish-brown above, paler below.
Range Found in Mexico, and also a small area of extreme S USA, in E Texas, SE Arizona and SW New Mexico.
Habitat Mostly in low grassy or scrub habitats, often in association with cotton rats and harvest mice. They are colonial and build their nest either below ground in a burrow or in a dense tangle of vegetation. They are mostly (though not exclusively) nocturnal.
Food Seeds and vegetation.

Breeding Almost all the year round; litters of 1-5, naked and blind young, weaned at just over 3 weeks.
Conservation Not threatened, but have only limited range in USA.
Similar Species None; most likely to be confused with Harvest Mice, which have grooved upper incisor.

Northern or Short-tailed Grasshopper Mouse

Onychomys leucogaster

Size TL 5-7½in (13-19cm);
T 1-2¼in (2.9-6.1cm);
WT 1-1¾oz (27-52g).

Identification Brownish to pinkish cinnamon or grayish
above, white below. The upper side of the tail is the same color
as the back at its base, but white-tipped. Other mice within its
range have longer tails. Aggressive and territorial; also vocal,
standing on hind legs when calling. Sounds audible to human
ear up to 330ft (100m) away.

Range Occurs over much of W North America from S
Canada to Mexico, except most of California and W Oregon.
Habitat Arid prairies and deserts, mostly associated with
sandy soils where they are most active on moonless nights.
Food Mostly grasshoppers, other insects, small mice,
scorpions, other animals and also some vegetable matter.
Breeding From May to October; 2-6 (usually 4) young,
naked and blind at birth. The juveniles have soft gray fur.
Conservation Not threatened.
Related Species Southern Grasshopper or Scorpion Mouse,
O. torridus, is smaller with a proportionally longer tail; it is
found in Mexico and north to S California, S Nevada, S Utah,
S Arizona and S New Mexico. Mearn's Grasshopper Mouse,
O. arenicoloris, found in Mexico and adjacent New Mexico.

Hispid Cotton Rat
Sigmodon hispidus

Size TL 8-14in (20.7-36.5cm);
T 3-6½in (7.5-16.6cm);
WT 2¾-4¼oz (80-120g).

Identification Coarse blackish or dark grizzled-brown fur above, grayer below; relatively short, scaly, almost hairless tail. Most other similar-sized rats are paler with longer tails.
Range Widespread in SE USA and south to Mexico.
Habitat Open grassy fields and shrubby areas, where they are often abundant.
Food Omnivorous, including vegetable matter, insects, crayfish and crabs, birds and their eggs, and also crops.
Breeding Extremely fecund, breeding at 6 weeks, and having several litters of 1-12 young which can be weaned at 5-7 days.

Conservation A serious pest of crops in many areas, including sugarcane and sweet potatoes.
Related Species Tawny-bellied Cotton Rat, *S. fulviventer*, which, as its name suggests, has a tawny belly; it is found in scattered populations in grasslands not grazed by domestic stock in SE Arizona, SW New Mexico and NW to central Mexico. Yellow-nosed Cotton Rat, *S. ochrognathus*, is also a mainly Mexican species, its range barely extending into the extreme S USA in a few areas of Texas, New Mexico and Arizona. It has a yellowish-orange muzzle.

Eastern Wood Rat
Neotoma floridana

Size TL 12-17in (31-44cm);
T 5-8in (12.9-20.3cm);
WT 7-16oz (200-455g).

Identification Gray-brown above, white below. The most obvious features of this species are the large houses they build from twigs, sticks, leaves and other materials, decorated with bottle tops, gun shells, and other items.
Range Widespread over much of E USA, particularly in SE, but absent from East Coast north of North Carolina.
Habitat Mostly rocky and wooded areas.
Food Mostly vegetable matter, storing seeds and nuts.
Breeding 2 or 3 litters a year, of 1-4 young.
Conservation Not threatened.

Related Species Southern Plains Woodrat, *N. micropus*, is confined to the Mexican/USA border area, north to S Kansas and S Colorado. **White-throated Woodrat,** *N. albigula*, which usually builds its house around cacti, is found from SE California to W Texas and Mexico. Desert Wood Rat, *N. lepida*, occurs from SE Oregon, Baja California, and Utah. Mexican Woodrat, *N. mexicana*, extends from Mexico north to S Utah and S Colorado. Dusky-footed Wood Rat, *N. fuscipes*, is found in West Coast from Oregon to Baja California; it often builds its houses high (over 49ft (15m)) in trees. Bushy-tailed Wood Rat or Pack Rat, *N. cinerea*, also builds in trees, but is most famous for its kleptomania for bright colored objects. It occurs throughout most of Rockies.

Southern Red-backed Vole
Clethrionomys gapperi

Size TL 4¾-6in (12-15.8cm);
T 1-1¾in (3-5cm);
WT ½-1½oz (16-42g).

Identification A small vole, with a short tail, and fairly
prominent ears. Reddish-brown fur on back, grayish on sides
and gray or silvery on underside. Distinguishes it from most
other voles. Often very numerous.
Range Widespread across North America, from S Canada, to
South Dakota and throughout Rockies of USA, New England
and south along Allegheny Mountains to North Carolina.

Habitat Forests (especially spruce and hemlock), woodlands,
bogs, and similar habitats with thick ground cover.
Food Green plants, shoots, mosses, seeds, berries, fungi; food
is cached in fall for use in winter.
Breeding Several litters a year from early spring to late fall.
2-8 (usually 3-4) young, born naked and helpless.
Conservation Not threatened.
Related Species Western Red-backed Vole, *C. californicus*
(*=occidentalis*) is found in coniferous forests in W USA from N
Oregon to N California. Northern Red-backed Vole, *C. rutilus*,
is found further north than Red-backed, in the tundra of
Canada and Alaska.

Heather Vole
Phenacomys intermedius

Size TL 4¾-6in (12 2-15.5cm);
T 1-1½in (2.6-4.1cm);
WT ½-1½oz (15-41g).

Identification Rather variable, but generally grizzled brown above and silvery below with a relatively short, sharply bicolored tail. Most likely to be confused with the Meadow Vole. *Phenacomys* Voles have roots to the cheek teeth, which are lacking in *Microtus* voles.

Range A wide, but not particularly well-known range across most of Canada and down the Rockies, to N California.
Habitat Often (but not exclusively) associated with red heather; also in coniferous forests.
Food A wide variety of bark, buds of shrubs, heathers and other vegetation, also lichens.
Breeding Breed from May to September in north of range; litter of 2-8, blind, naked, and helpless young.
Conservation Little known but not as rare as once thought.
Related Species Red Tree Vole, *P. longicaudus*, is a rather arboreal species, superficially similar to red-backed voles, found only in coastal Oregon and California. White-footed Vole, *P. albipes*, is one of the rarest of N American small mammals restricted to coastal Oregon, and possibly NW California. Dusky Tree Vole, *P. silvicola*, is a rather dark arboreal vole, is restricted to central coastal Oregon.

Field Voles
Microtus spp

½in
(1cm)

Size TL 4-10¼in (10.1-26.5cm);
T ½-4½in (1.7-11.5cm);
WT ¾-3½oz (20-103g).

Identification Most *Microtus* voles are grayish, and their ears
are rather small, often largely hidden in fur. Their tails are
short, the soles of their feet hairless, and their cheek teeth do
not have roots. The populations of several species are cyclic,
building up and crashing at regular intervals, depending on
food availability. Many of the species can only be identified
with certainty by detailed measurement and tooth characters,
but range is also a useful aid to identification.

Range The most widespread and often abundant within its
range is the **Meadow Vole,** *M. pennsylvanicus*, from Alaska to
Labrador and south through Rockies, across to south of Great
Lakes, and down Appalachians. The closely related Muskeget
Meadow Vole, *M. breweri* is confined to Muskeget Island,
Massachusetts. Mountain Vole, *M. montanus*, is a widespread
but little-studied species found in Rockies from British
Columbia south to Arizona and New Mexico. California Vole,
M. californicus, is confined to California and SW Oregon and
Baja California. Townsend's Vole, *M. townsendi*, is confined to
moist grassy habitats in West Coast America from Vancouver
Island south to NW California. **Tundra Vole,** *M. oeconomus*,
is found in NW Canada and Alaska. It is also found across the
tundra of Siberia and west to Europe, where it is known as the
Root Vole. Long-tailed Vole, *M. longicaudus*, is a large vole
with a range which extends from SE Alaska south to central
California and east to Nevada and New Mexico; there is an
isolated population in Black Hills, South Dakota. The closely
related Coronation Island Vole, *M. coronarius*, is confined to
Coronation Island off British Columbia. Mexican Vole,
M. mexicanus, is found from N Mexico into USA either side of
the Arizona-New Mexico border. Rock Vole, *M. chrotorrhinus*,
has a distinctive yellowish muzzle; it is found in E Canada and
south along Appalachians to N Carolina. Yellow-cheeked Vole,
M. xanthognathus, has an orange muzzle, but its range is quite
separate; it occurs in NW Canada and central Alaska in
forests. Oregon or Creeping Vole, *M. oregoni*, is confined to
coastal Oregon, S British Columbia, Washington, and N
California. Singing or Alaska Vole, *M. gregalis*, is colonial and
confined to Alaska and adjacent Canada; it takes its name

from its habit of standing at the entrance to its burrow and making a high-pitched trilling sound. Prairie Vole, *M. ochrogaster*, is found from S Canada (Alberta to Manitoba) south to Louisiana and has been found in Texas, but is now believed extinct. Pine or Woodland Vole, *M. pinetorum*, is widespread over much of E North America from central Texas, north to Great Lakes, extreme SE Canada, and west to N Florida and New England; it is absent from most areas.

Meadow Vole

Habitat Found in a wide variety of mostly grassland habitats, including prairies, marshes and woodland clearings. They make runs and tunnels among roots and stems. Nests of grasses, shredded bark, usually below or at ground level, often underlogs, rocks.

Food Mostly vegetable matter, particularly grasses, forbs, sedges, twigs, roots, bulbs. Some species take small amounts of animal matter.

Breeding Most species have several litters a year of up to 12 young. The young are blind, naked, and helpless at birth, but develop rapidly, and often mature within a few weeks.

Conservation Some populations of a few species are endangered, and many others are rare or little known. However, they are mostly abundant and prolific mammals.

Similar Species Other voles can be difficult to distinguish, even at close range.

Tundra Vole

Water Vole
Arvicola richardsoni

Size TL 7¾-10¼in (19.8-26.1cm);
T 2½-3½in (6.9- 9.2cm);
WT 2½-3½oz (70-98g).

Identification One of the largest North American voles, with long, grayish to reddish-brown fur above, paler below. Its tail is relatively long and bicolored and there are fringes of hair on the feet. Swims well.
Range A relatively small range, confined to the Rockies of south Canada and N USA.
Habitat Restricted to streams, rivers, and lakes, usually in alpine meadows, but also in woodlands and forest glades, where it excavates extensive burrows. In winter it may move away from water and build its nest under snow.
Food Mostly vegetable matter, including roots, twigs, shoots, and buds (particularly willows), and grasses.
Breeding Usually 2 litters a year of 2-8 (average 5) young, born naked, blind, and helpless.
Conservation Not threatened.
Similar Species Not likely to be confused with any other vole; most other similar-sized rodents have longer tails.

Sagebrush Vole
Lagurus curtatus

Size TL 4¼-5½in (10.8-14.2cm);
T ½-1¼in (1.6-2.8cm);
WT ½-1¼oz (17-38g).

Identification A small vole, pale gray above, whitish below, with a short furry tail, with a dark stripe along its top. It is not likely to be confused with any other vole; all others are larger, darker, with longer tails; it is also usually the only vole found within its habitat.
Range In Rockies from Washington and SW Manitoba to extreme E California, Nevada and S Utah.
Habitat Mostly in mature sagebrush steppes, semi-arid prairies, generally with loose soils. It builds its nest at the base of shrubs, and excavates shallow runways to nearby shrubs.

Food Mostly leaves of sagebrush and also woody parts. Feed by day as well as at night.
Breeding They live in loose colonies and in the south breed all the year round, and may have more than one litter a year of 1-13 (usually 3-6) young.
Conservation Not threatened.
Similar Species Most likely to be confused other voles.

Round-tailed Muskrat
Neofiber alleni

Size TL 11-15in (28.5-38.1cm);
T 3¾-6½in (9.9-16.8cm);
WT 5½-12¼oz (155-350g).

Identification Like a small muskrat, dark brown above, buff or almost white below. The tail is round, naked and scaly, and the hind feet slightly webbed. Only likely to be confused with the Muskrat which is larger, has a flattened tail, and differs in range.
Range Confined to Florida and SE Georgia.
Habitat In a wide range of aquatic habitats, preferring those with a water depth of 6-18in (15-46cm). They build dome-shaped lodges from grasses and other vegetation. It is nocturnal and generally rather less aquatic than the Muskrat.
Food Aquatic and other vegetation, including roots and tubers, feeding mostly at night.
Breeding They breed all year round, but mostly in late fall and winter. There are 4-6 litters of 1-4 young, naked, blind, and helpless at birth. They grow rapidly and are swimming and feeding within a fortnight.

Conservation Not threatened. Locally cause some damage to agriculture, and undermine canal banks.
Similar Species Muskrat. Brown Rat has a more pointed snout, and does not build lodges.

Muskrat
Ondatra zibethicus

1³/₄ in (4.5cm)

Size TL 16-25in (40.6-64.1cm);
T 7-11½in (17.7-29.5cm);
WT 1-4¼lbs (541g-1.95kg).

Identification A large, stocky, blunt-headed rodent, with a long, nearly naked, vertically flattened, scaly tail. Dark glossy brown above, lighter on the side and pale on the underside. The hind feet are partially webbed. It builds large lodges, similar to those of beavers, from aquatic plants, particularly cattails, on a platform of mud and other vegetation.
Range Widespread over most of North America from Alaska, across most of Canada (except areas more or less permanently frozen) south throughout most of USA except the arid areas of the south. Also absent from Florida and Georgia.

Habitat Almost any aquatic habitats.
Food Mostly aquatic vegetation, including
cattails, rushes, pondweeds, water lilies, sedges. They also eat crayfish, clams, frogs and fish. The food is eaten on a flattened feeding platform, where the remains are a good indication of the Muskrats' presence.
Breeding One to 5 litters a year of 1-11 (usually 4-7) young which are born naked, blind, and helpless. They grow rapidly and are furred, diving and swimming at about 2 weeks.
Conservation An important fur bearer; also causes damage to agriculture, undermines river and canal banks.
Similar Species Round-tailed Muskrat. Distinguished from Beaver by its smaller size and round, slender tail.

Brown Lemming
Lemnus trimucronatus (=sibiricus)

Size TL 5-6½in (13.2-16.8cm);
T ½-1in (1.6-2.6cm);
WT 1½-4oz (41-113g).

Identification A small vole-like rodent with reddish-brown fur, grayer on head, and longer and grayer in winter. It is specialized for digging with the soles of its feet covered in long, stiff hairs, and broad and curved claws. Their populations are cyclic, peaking every 3-4 years then crashing.
Range Found from Alaskan Peninsula eastward across Alaska and Arctic Canada to western shores of Hudson's Bay; south through Rockies to N British Columbia. Also occurs in NE Siberia and Kamchatka, USSR.

Habitat Found in tundra and alpine meadows, where they make extensive surface burrows, tunnel under boulders, where nests made of fine grasses, lined with fur, are made. Surface nests are also built.
Food Grasses, sedges, forbs and other green plants in summer; twigs (particularly dwarf birch and willows) in winter.
Breeding One to 3 litters a year of 4-9 (average 7) young, born naked, blind, and helpless.
Conservation Not threatened.
Similar Species Likely to be confused with voles.

Southern Bog Lemming
Synaptomys cooperi

Size TL 4½-6in (11.5-15.8cm);
T ½-1in (1.3-2.7cm);
WT ¾-1¾oz (21-50g).

Identification A small vole, with relatively long fur; grizzled brown on the back, grading to silvery gray on the underside. Its eyes are small and ears largely covered with fur. Distinguished from voles by its extremely short tail, and grooves on its upper incisor teeth. The scats are usually bright green.

Range Occurs from Kansas to Manitoba, and east to Quebec and North Carolina, often at low densities.
Habitat Mostly grassy meadows; its name is misleading, particularly in the south of its range, where it it is found in woodland clearings and old fields, with thick grass cover.
Food Leaves, seeds of grasses, sedges, mosses, fungi, and some insects.
Breeding From early spring to late summer, with several litters a year of 3-5 young, born naked, blind, and helpless.
Conservation Sparse, isolated populations.
Related Species Northern Bog Lemming, *S. borealis*, has a wide, but poorly known distribution across most of N Canada and Alaska, and south into N Washington, N Idaho and N Montana. It can usually be distinguished from Southern Bog Lemming by buff-orange fur at the base of the ears.

Collared Lemming
*Dicrostonyx groenlandicus
(=torquatus)*

Size TL 5-6¼in (13.2-16.2cm);
T ¼-¾in (1-2cm);
WT 2-4oz (56-112g).

Identification The only rodent in North America to turn
white in winter. In summer, grayish buff above with a black
stripe down the middle, gray or whitish below, with a chestnut
or buff chest.
Range Only found in the extreme north of North America,
from western shores of Hudson's Bay to the Alaska Peninsula.
Habitat Arctic tundra.
Food Grasses, sedges bear berry in summer, and twigs of
dwarf willow and other shrubs in winter; but also almost any
available vegetation when numbers peak.
Breeding Two or 3 litters a year of 1-7 (usually 3) young.
Conservation Not threatened. A major food item for many
Arctic predators, including Arctic Fox, Snowy Owl,
Wolverines and Wolf.
Related Species Ungava or Labrador Lemming, *D.
hudsonius*, is found on eastern shores of Hudson's Bay, east to
Labrador. Distinguished by skull differences, but is also paler.

Black Rat
Rattus rattus

Size TL 12-17in (32.5-45.5cm);
T 6¼-10in (16-25.5cm);
WT 4-12¼oz (115-350g).

Identification Similar in general appearance to the familiar
Brown Rat, but with a proportionally longer tail and more
prominent ears. Coloring very variable, black animals are
common, but various shades of brown, gray or buff also occur.
Rice rats are very similar but have bicolored tails; woodrats
have white undersides.

Range A native of Asia, it has spread to Europe and thence to
the New World. It is most abundant and widespread in coastal
areas to SW British Columbia and Maine, but is rare in many
inland areas, such as Arizona.

Habitat Ubiquitous, but generally associated with human
habitations, agricultural areas, and habitats heavily modified
by man. Often abundant around seaports, where they continue
to be reintroduced. They are agile climbers, both in trees and
in houses.

Food Omnivorous scavengers.
Breeding Prolific, producing several litters a year of 2-10
young (usually 7 or 8), blind, naked, and helpless at birth.
Conservation Pest.
Similar Species Most likely to be confused with Brown Rat,
Rice Rats or Woodrats.

Brown Rat
Rattus norvegicus

Size TL 12-18in (31.6-46cm);
T 4¾-9in (12.2-23cm);
WT 5-17½oz (140-500g).

Identification The common rat, unfortunately familiar in most urban, suburban, and rural environments. Grayish brown, with a greasy sheen to fur, above and paler below. Its tail is naked and scaly, proportionally shorter than that of Black Rat.

Range Widespread across all USA and Mexico and north to S Canada, extending further north in coastal areas. In some areas it is uncommon - for instance Arizona.

Habitat Almost always associated with human habitations, farmland, farm buildings. It is an excellent swimmer, often inhabiting canals and sewers.

Food Omnivorous, eating almost anything with any nutritional value, and often causing enormous damage to stored foods.

Breeding Up to 12 litters a year of 2-22 (usually 7-11) young, born naked, blind, and helpless.

Conservation Major pest.

Similar Species Most likely to be confused with Black Rat, Rice Rats, Woodrats and possibly Round-tailed Muskrat.

House Mouse
Mus domesticus

Size TL 5-7¾in (13-19.8cm);
T 2½-4in (6.3-10.2cm);
WT 16-25g.

Identification The most familiar small rodent over most of
North America. Generally gray or grayish brown above, often
only slightly paler below. The long, slender tail is nearly naked.
Most likely to be confused with harvest mice which have
grooves on their teeth (lacking in House Mouse) or deer mice
which have larger eyes and white undersides.
Range Over most of North America from S Canada
southward.
Habitat Mostly in and around human habitations, farmlands
and open scrubby habitats.

Food Mostly seeds, particularly weed seed, but in and around
domestic and agricultural buildings do immense amount of
damage to stored foodstuff.
Breeding Extremely prolific; up to 13 littters a year of 3-12
(average 6) young, born naked, blind, and helpless, that are
sexually mature at 6-8 weeks.
Conservation Pest.
Related Species Normally regarded as a single species, but
recent research in Europe has shown that there are probably
more than 6 closely related species in the Old World; some
may occur in North America.

Meadow Jumping Mouse
Zapus hudsonius

Size TL 7¼-10in (18.7-25.5cm);
T 3-6in (10.8-15.5cm);
WT 13-28g.

Identification A small mouse with a long tail (over half total length), which is dark above, pale below, with yellowish sides. Well-developed hindlegs; when startled, makes a few bounding jumps, then freezes.
Range Ranges across North America from S Alaska through Canada to Labrador and Nova Scotia, extending south in east as far as N Oklahoma and N Georgia.

Habitat A wide variety of open habitats including meadow, forest edge, grassland, and marsh, often swimming. They hibernate for up to 8 months, in a nest in a hollow log or among roots, usually above ground level.
Food Seeds, grasses, green plants, and fungi and also beetles, grubs and other insects.
Breeding 2 or 3 litters a year of 2-8 (4-6) young, born naked and helpless.
Conservation Not threatened, but uncommon or rare over much of its range.
Related Species Western Jumping Mouse, *Z. princeps*, is widespread, larger and more yellow on the sides than the Meadow Jumping Mouse. Pacific Jumping Mouse, *Z. trinolatus*, is closely related and confined to West Coast from S British Columbia to N California, best identified by its range.

Woodland Jumping Mouse
Neozapus insignis

Size TL 8-10in (20.4-25.9cm);
T 4½-6¼in (11.5-16cm);
WT 17-31.5g.

Identification An elegant, attractive little mouse. Very similar to the three species of Meadow Mice, but has a distinctive white tip to long, thin tail. It is rather brightly colored, brownish on the back with buff-orange sides and white underparts. Distinguished from Meadow Jumping Mice by habitat. Can jump 10-13ft (3-4m). Hibernates from late Sept-early May in north, Nov-April in south.
Range NE North America from around Great Lakes north to coast of Labrador, east to New England and New York, and south along Appalachians to NE Georgia, where it is only found at altitudes of over 2788ft (850m).
Habitat Spruce forests, hemlock forests and other well-wooded habitats; also bogs swamps, but rarely open fields and meadows. They are sociable and appear to live in loose colonies. Although rarely seen, they are sometimes abundant.

Food A wide range of plants and insects.
Breeding One or 2 litters a year of 2-7 (usually 3-4) young, born naked, blind, and helpless.
Conservation Not threatened.
Similar Species Meadow Jumping Mice.

Porcupine
Erethizon dorsatum

Size: TL 2-3ft (64.8-93cm);
T 5¾-11¾in (14.8-30cm);
WT 7¾-39½lbs (3.5-18kg).

Identification Unmistakable. The only mammal in North America largely covered with spiny quills. In east it is blackish brown, in west more yellowish. It is arboreal and mostly nocturnal, but its presence can be detected by scats (rather deer-like) and patches of bark stripped from trees, neatly gnawed twigs and branches, with prominent tooth marks. The footprint is also distinctive.
Range Widespread over most of N and W North America, south as far as Pennsylvania in the east.
Habitat Woodland and forest.
Food Leaves, twigs and bark of trees; also green plants including lupines, clovers and crops such as alfalfa and corn.
Breeding A single young born early late spring or summer; the quills are soft at birth but harden within about 15 mins.
Conservation Not threatened; where they are abundant can cause considerable damage to trees, frequently killing parts of a tree by ring-barking it.
Similar Species None in North America.

Nutria or Coypu
Myocastor coypus

3³/₄in
(9.5cm)

Size TL 2-4½ft (67-1.4m);
T 10-17in (25.5-44cm);
WT 5-37½lbs (2.3-17kg).

Identification A large aquatic rodent with a long scaly tail. Most likely to be confused with Beaver, which is larger with a flat, paddle-shaped tail, or Muskrat, which is smaller with a vertically flattened tail. Nutrias do not build lodges like Beavers or Muskrats.

Range A native of South America, introduced into North America as a fur-bearer. Now widespread in Louisiana and adjacent states, and scattered populations in other states, notably the Pacific Northwest.

Habitat Swamps, marshes, canals, ponds.

Food Almost exclusively vegetarian; terrestrial and aquatic vegetation.

Breeding All the year round; 1-11 (usually 4-6) young born well developed and actively swimming within 24 hours.

Conservation Non-native; important fur-bearer in many areas; pest causing extensive damage to agriculture in a few areas, raiding crops and undermining canal and stream banks.

Similar Species None; most likely to be mistaken for Muskrat or Beaver.

Coyote
Canis latrans

2½ in
(6 cm)

Size TL 3¼-4¾ft (1-1.5m);
T 12-15in (30-40cm);
SH c2ft (58-66cm);
WT 20-42lbs (9.1-18.1kg).

Identification Gray or reddish gray, with bushy, dark-tipped tail, held low when running. Smaller than the Wolf and has a smaller nose pad (less than 1in (2.5cm) diameter) and larger and grayer than Red Fox. Most likely confused with dogs, in particular "coydogs" - hybrids between coyotes and dogs. Voice varies, but most characteristic is a series of yapping barks followed by a howl and ending in short "yipping," usually heard at dusk or dawn.

Range One of the most widespread mammals in North America, found in all mainland US states and most of Canada, except extreme north.

Habitat Ubiqitous, but most often abundant in open plains and scrubby areas; has spread into suburbs of many towns.

Food Carrion, insects, melons, rodents, rabbits, turtles, domestic poultry, gophers, frogs; they sometimes hunt in small groups to catch larger prey such as deer.

Breeding One litter a year of 1-9 (usually 6) young, born blind and helpless.

Conservation Widely regarded as a pest, but generally increasing.

Similar Species Wolf, Red Fox and dogs.

Gray Wolf
Canis lupus

4 in
(10 cm)

Size TL 4-5¾ft (1.3-1.8m);
T 13-19in (35-50cm);
SH 2-3ft (66-97cm);
WT 57¼-129¾lbs (26-59kg).

Identification A large carnivore, superficially similar to the domestic German Shepherd, but grayer with a bushier, straighter, black-tipped tail. However the color is variable, ranging from snowy white to almost black, and also yellowish or reddish brown. Most likely to be confused with Coyote, which is smaller. Wolves howl and bark, and will respond to humans imitating them.

Range Formerly widespread over North America, except the SE; now confined to Alaska, Canada and a few of the co-terminous USA, around Great Lakes and in Rockies.

Habitat Forests and tundra.

Food Mostly mammals up to size of Moose and Caribou, including domestic stock. Also smaller animals and some fruit.

Breeding Wolves live in packs, averaging about 8. A single litter of 1-11 (usually 6-7) young, blind and helpless.

Conservation Extinct or endangered over most of its range, but still widespread and relatively abundant in the more remote parts of Canada and Alaska.

Related Species Red Wolf, *C. rufus*, similar to Gray Wolf but smaller and more rufous. It had a wide range in SE USA, from Pennsylvania to Florida and Texas, but by 1970s was extinct in the wild. Captive bred animals are being reintroduced.

Arctic Fox
Alopex lagopus

2⅛ in
(5.5 cm)

Size TL 2½-3ft (75-91cm);
T 10½-13in (27-35cm);
SH 9¾-11¾in (25-30cm);
WT 5½-8¾lbs (2.5-4kg).

Identification A very variable, often colonial fox. Its pelage varies from brown to blue gray or grayish white in summer, in winter it is white or yellowish white. It is slightly smaller than the Red Fox, with shorter, more rounded ears, and a bushier, more uniformly colored tail.

Range Confined to Alaska and N Canada. Introduced on several of the Aleutian Islands. Also widespread in the northern regions of the Old World.

Habitat Tundra and the edges of Arctic forests. Excavates burrows which may be used for many centuries and occupy a large area.

Food Lemmings, voles, nesting birds, birds' eggs, fruit, and frequently scavenge Polar Bear kills. Populations are cyclical following abundance of voles and lemmings. They make caches of food.

Breeding A litter of 1-14 (usually 5 or 6, and record is 25) born blind and helpless in spring.

Conservation Not threatened.

Similar Species Only likely to be confused with Red Fox.

Red Fox
Vulpes fulva (=vulpes)

Size TL 2¾-3½ft (82cm-1.15m);
T 11¼-17in (29-45.5cm);
SH 16in (38-41cm);
WT 6½-15½lbs (3-7kg).

2 in
(5 cm)

Identification A small dog-like mammal, generally reddish brown above with white underparts and a long, white-tipped bushy tail. The feet and backs of the ears are blackish. However the pelage is very variable and almost black. Individuals occur as well as silver and "cross" - with a dark marking on the shoulder.
Range Widespread over most of Canada, Alaska and most of USA except south-west.
Habitat Occurs in a wide range of habitats, including woodlands, forest, farmland, and scrubby hillsides, to Arctic tundra; they also occur in suburbs on golf couses and cemetaries.
Food Small mammals, birds, fruit, insects, often storing food such as mice and rabbits in caches.
Breeding One litter a year of 1-10 (usually 5-7) young, born blind and helpless. The dens are usually burrows, among rock clefts.
Conservation Not threatened.
Similar Species Most likely to be mistaken for other foxes or domestic dogs, but none have white tip to tail.

Swift Fox
Vulpes velox

Size TL 2-2¾ft (60-88cm);
T 9-13in (23-35cm);
WT 3-6lbs (1.4-2.7kg).

1¾ in
(4.5 cm)

Identification A small gray fox with extremely large ears. It has a fairly uniform coloring, grayish yellow above, paler below, with a black tip to the tail. The Gray and Red Foxes are less uniform, with smaller ears.
Range From S Alberta, Saskatchewan and Manitoba, to N Texas and W New Mexico.
Habitat Confined to open shortgrass prairies and similar arid habitats; also cultivated areas and range lands. Mostly nocturnal, spending the day in burrows.
Food Small rodents, rabbits, birds, insects and some vegetable matter including berries and grasses. Caches food in winter, under snow.
Breeding A single litter born in spring, 3-6 young born blind and helpless.
Conservation Numbers became much reduced as a result of poisoning by baits set for Coyotes. Since the 1950s increasing has been noted over much of their former range.
Related Species Kit Fox, *V. macrotis*, is slightly smaller than Swift Fox, and found in the SW, and north to S Oregon and formerly SW Idaho; in Oregon and California the populations are fragmented and isolated.

Gray Fox
Urocyon cinereoargenteus

Size TL 2½-3½ft (80cm-1.12m);
T 8½-17in (22-44cm); SH 14in (36-38cm);
WT 7¼-15½lbs (3.3-7kg).

1¾ in
(4.5 cm)

Identification Distinguished from other foxes by distinctive, colorful pelage. Its back is gray with a grizzled "salt-and-pepper" appearance, the underside and base of ears are orange or buff, with a white throat, chest band and on the insides of legs. Red Fox has a white-tipped tail.

Range Widespread in E and S USA, the extreme SE Canada but absent from much of the Plains and Rockies, range also extends south through Mexico to Central and South America, and north through California and Oregon.

Habitat Variable, but often in fairly well-wooded habitats, or with scrubby brush and dense cover. Generally rather arboreal, foraging in trees, and often taking refuge in trees when pursued, often seen by day.

Food Omnivorous; small mammals, nesting birds, insects, and vegetable matter, particularly fruit.

Breeding A single litter, born in spring, of 1-7 (usually 4) young, born blind and helpless. The den is usually in a rock cleft, hollow tree in a thicket, or even in a beaver lodge.

Conservation Not threatened.

Related Species Island Fox, *U. littoralis*, is a diminutive version of Gray Fox, confined to the Californian islands of Santa Miguel, Santa Rosa, Santa Cruz, San Nicolas, San Clemente and Santa Catalina.

Black Bear
Ursus americanus

7 in
(18 cm)

Size TL 4½-6ft (1.37-1.88m);
T 3-6¾in (7.7-17.7cm);
\SH 3-3¼ft (90cm-1.05m);
WT 88--660lbs (40-300kg).

Identification Fairly unmistakable: the Black Bear is blackish in east, but more variable in west, often brownish cinnamon, with a white chest patch. Whitish and bluish phases occur in Northwest. Signs of bears' presence are often overturned logs, mammal burrows dug up, branches and twigs broken.
Range Occurs over most of Canada, south through Rockies to California and Mexico, and along East Coast to Florida; isolated populations elsewhere.
Habitat Mostly woodlands and forests, also in swamps, mountains. It hibernates, even in the south of its range.
Food Omnivorous; varies according to season; insects and grubs, small mammals (rabbits, mice, voles, squirrels), berries, leaves, shoots, carrion, fish. Also crops, particularly honey.
Breeding Litter born late winter or early spring; 1-5 (usually 2-3) are tiny, naked, blind and helpless at birth. Den in a rock-cleft, cave, among tree roots.
Conservation Although once declining in most parts of its range it is now protected and/or managed throughout most of its range. Reintroduced in many reserves and protected areas. Locally a pest, causing damage to apiaries.
Similar Species Grizzly Bear.

Grizzly Bear
Ursus arctos

10 in (25 cm)

Size TL 6-7ft (1.8-2.13m);
T 3in (7.6cm); SH 4¼ft (1.3m);
WT 323-849lbs (147-386kg)
(exceptionally heavier).

Identification A large bear, usually brownish or yellowish brown, with pale guard hairs giving a grizzled appearance. Signs are similar to those of Black Bear, but since they are larger, claw marks are often higher on trees.
Range Confined to Alaska and NW Canada, with isolated populations further south in Rockies, south to Yellowstone National Park.
Habitat Relatively open country, often in mountainous regions.
Food Omnivorous, and variable according to season and local availability; includes fish (particularly spent salmon in fall), berries, grass (in spring), carrion, rodents, and large mammals up to size of deer, and domestic livestock.
Breeding Litters born alternate year in early spring; 1-4 (usually 2) young are born naked, blind, and helpless. Den in a cave, among tree roots.
Conservation Range considerably reduced, and extinct over much of its former range in USA and Mexico; still widespread and abundant in many parts of NW Canada and Alaska.
Similar Species Only likely to be confused with Black Bear.

Polar Bear
Ursus maritimus

12 in
(30 cm)

Size TL 7-8ft (2.13-2.5m);
T 3-5in (8-13cm);
SH 3¾ft (1.2m);
WT 330-1100lbs (150-500kg, occasionally up to 650kg).

Identification Quite unmistakable. A large bear pure white or yellowish white with a black nose.
Range In North America, confined to Arctic slope of Alaska and Canada; also in the Old World Arctic.
Habitat Almost entirely confined to coastal areas and pack ice, where it is an expert swimmer.
Food Mammals, particularly Ringed Seals, also scavenging whale carcasses, birds and their eggs, crustaceans, and also berries and grasses when available .
Breeding Litters are born at intervals of 2-4 years, in mid-winter, in the den. The 1-3 young are blind, naked, and helpless at birth.
Conservation Once seriously threatened, but under strict protection numbers have recovered in most areas.
Similar Species None.

Ringtail or Cacomistle
Bassariscus astutus

1¹⁄₈ in
(3 cm)

Size TL 2-2¹⁄₂ft (61.6-81.1cm);
T 12-17in (30.5-43.8cm);
WT 26¹⁄₂-38³⁄₄lbs (750gm-1.1kg).

Identification A slender, rather cat-like carnivore, gray or
yellowish gray above, buff below with a long bushy tail,
banded alternately black and white. Only likely to be confused
with the Coati, which has a thinner, less distinctly banded tail,
or Raccoon, which is larger, more thick-set with a shorter tail,
and has a characteristic face-mask. Normally nocturnal,
denning in a hollow tree or among rocks. Extremely agile.
When cornered emit a foul-smelling scent from the anal gland.
Range From SW Oregon south to Mexico and east to
Oklahoma, Kansas and Texas, at altitudes of up to 9186ft
(2800m).

Habitat Usually in rocky areas with cliffs, canyons, talus
slopes, in chaparral or woodland, usually near water.
Food Small mammals, large insects (crickets and
grasshoppers), scorpions, carrion, fruit, berries, reptiles and
amphibians.
Breeding A single (possibly more) litter born in late spring of
summer; 2-4 young, blind and helpless.
Conservation Not threatened.
Related Species Coati, *Nasua nasua*, often called the
Coatimundi, is found in the extreme SW USA and Mexico. It
is larger and less attractively marked than the Ringtail.

Raccoon
Procyon lotor

3 in
(7.5 cm)

Size TL 2-3ft (60.3-95cm);
T 7½-16in (19.2-40.6cm);
WT 8-19¾lbs (3.6-9kg, exceptionally up to 28.3kg).

Identification One of the most familiar carnivores in North America; generally dark grayish or grayish brown above, paler below. It is easily identified by the stiped tail and black face-mask. Nocturnal and crepuscular, and a frequent roadkill. Swims and climbs well.

Range Widespread over North America from S Canada, throughout most of USA to Mexico, except for some areas in Rockies and Great Basin.
Habitat Almost ubiquitous within range, provided there is water available; most abundant along well-wooded streams, mangroves. Often in suburbs.
Food Omnivorous, including fruit, berries, crabs, crayfish, frogs, birds and their eggs, insects, turtle eggs, rodents, carrions and also raids garbage cans.
Breeding Usually a single litter in late spring; 1-8 (usually 2-5), born blind and helpless.
Conservation Not threatened; carries rabies in some areas; an important fur-bearer and widely hunted for sport.
Similar Species Not likely to be confused with any other species.

Pine Marten
Martes americana

Size TL 20-25in (51.3-65.9cm);
T 5¼-9¼in (13.5-24cm);
WT 15¾-55¼oz (448g-1.57kg).

1³/₄ in
(4.5 cm)

Identification A large weasel-like carnivore varying from dark glossy brown to yellowish above, paler below, with a buff or orange throat patch. Most likely to be confused with Fisher which is larger and lacks throat patch, or mink which is smaller, darker, with shorter tail.
Range Occurs widely across Canada to Alaska and south through Rockies to N California in West and to New York and New England in East.
Habitat Almost exclusively forests, particularly conifers.
Food Small mammals, birds, insects, and fruit.
Breeding Young born in spring; 1-5 (usually 2-4) young, born blind, naked, and helpless in a nest built in a tree.
Conservation After declining in many areas, particularly in E USA and Canada, now increasing; reintroduction programs in many places.
Similar Species Most likely to be confused with Fisher.

Fisher
Martes pennanti

2 in (5 cm)

Size TL 2½-3¼ft (79cm- 1.03m);
T 12-16in (30-42cm);
WT 7¾ -11lbs (3.5-5.kg, exceptionally to over 9kg).

Identification A large dark brown weasel distingushed from the Marten by its larger size and lack of throat patch.
Range Similar to that of the Marten though less widespread. It occurs across Canada and south into USA with scattered populations in Rockies and north-east, as far south as New York.
Habitat Variable, but usually dependent on mature forests.
Food Wide range of mostly animal prey including small rodents, porcupines, snowshoe hares, and carrion (deer, beaver), also birds, eggs, fruits, and nuts.

Breeding One to 5 (usually 2-5) young, born blind and helpless, in a nest in rock cleft, tree hollow.
Conservation Like Marten, suffered considerable reduction in range during 19th and early 20th centuries; now carefully managed, and several reintroduction programs.
Similar Species Only likely to be confused with Marten.

Short-tailed Weasel or Ermine
Mustela erminea

Size TL 7½-13in (19-34cm);
T 1½-3½in (4.2-9cm);
WT 1½-6½oz (45-182g).

Identification A medium-sized weasel, the males are 30% larger than females. It is brown above, creamy white below and has a black-tipped tail (which distinguishes it from the Least Weasel), and white feet (which distinguishes it from the Long-tailed Weasel). In winter, in the northern parts of its range it molts into an all-white pelage, except for the black tail-tip. They can be "squeaked."

Range Widespread across most of Canada (except northern Prairies) and Alaska and south in Rockies, around Great Lakes and New England to Pennsylvania and Maryland.

Habitat Wide range of habitats including open woodlands, farmlands, tundra, and marshes.

Food Exclusively carnivorous, feeding mostly on mice and voles, but also birds, shrews, squirrels, young rabbits, and occasionally amphibians and fish.

Breeding A single litter of 6-9 young, born blind and helpless, but covered in fine fur. The den is usually in a burrow, under rocks or logs.

Conservation Not threatened.

Similar Species Most likely to be confused with other weasels.

Least Weasel
Mustela nivalis

Size TL 6¾-8in (17.2-20.6cm);
T ¾-1½in (2.4-3.8cm);
WT 1¼-1¾oz (37-50g).

Identification A small weasel, and one of the smallest carnivores in the world. It is brown above, white below and the short tail does not have a black tip. In winter (except in the south of its range) it turns completely white. Can be "squeaked."
Range Occurs across N North America from Alaska to Labrador, and south as far as northern prairies (W Montana) and east to S Appalachians.
Habitat Varied, but grassy fields, pastures, open woodlands, often close to rivers, marshes.
Food Carnivorous, feeding mostly on mice, voles, small rabbits, water voles, also birds, and other animals.
Breeding 2-3 litters occurring most months of the year, particularly in south of range; 3-6 young, born blind and helpless.
Conservation Not threatened.
Similar Species Only likely to be confused with Short-tailed Weasel.

Long-tailed Weasel
Mustela frenata

Size TL 11-22in (28-55cm);
T 3-6¼in (8-16cm);
WT 3-9¼oz (85-267g).

1¼in
(3cm)

Identification A medium-sized weasel (males twice the size of females) weasel. Brown or yellowish brown above, with a brown, black-tipped tail and brown feet; white to rusty orange on the underside. Some populations (Florida and South-west) may have pale facial markings. In winter in northern latitudes it molts into entirely white pelage, except for black tail tip. Over much of USA some molt, while others stay brown. Separated from other weasels by size, and long tail; from Black-footed Ferret by coloring and markings.
Range Widespread over most of USA, except extreme Southwest, extending into extreme S Canada, and also south through Central America to Bolivia.
Habitat Very varied, including forests, marshes, open grasslands and farmlands, usually fairly close to water.

Food Carnivorous feeding mostly on small mammals including rabbits, squirrels, voles, mice and also poultry and other small birds and animals.
Breeding A single litter, in mid-late summer, of 6-9 young, born blind and helpless.
Conservation Not threatened.
Similar Species Only likely to be confused with other weasels or Black-footed Ferret.

Black-footed Ferret
Mustela nigripes

Size TL 18-22in (48-57.3cm);
T 4½-5½in (11.4-13.9cm);
WT 18¾-45¾oz (535g-1.3kg).

Identification A medium-sized weasel, the males are larger than females. It is superficially similar in appearance to the domestic ferret sold in pet stores. Upper parts are buff, underparts and face paler, with a raccoon-like, black face-mask, black feet, and black tail-tip.

Range Once widespread in the Plains states from extreme S Sasketchewan to Texas; now probably extinct in the wild. Rewards offered for sightings in some states.
Habitat Shortgrass prairies, almost exclusively associated with prairie dog towns.
Food Mammals, particularly prairie dogs, and other animals.
Breeding A single litter in spring; 3-5 young born, blind and helpless, in a den underground.
Conservation Has been declared extinct on several occasions, but survives through captive breeding activities; reintroductions are planned.
Similar Species Most likely to be confused with Long-tailed Weasel.

Mink
Mustela vison

Size TL 18-28in (48.1-72cm);
T 5½-9¼in (14.4-23.8cm);
WT 1½-3½lbs (630g-1.6kg).

1⅛ in
(3 cm)

Identification A fairly large weasel, the males are larger than females. It is distinguished from other weasels by its coloring, which is usually a uniform dark glossy brown or almost black, with a small amount of white on the chin and throat.
Range Found over almost all of Canada and USA except the arid South-west.
Habitat Esssentially aquatic and never found far from water, in marshes, swamps, ponds, lakes, and rivers.
Food A wide variety of animals including blackbirds, frogs, crayfish, fish, deer mice, and rabbits.

Breeding Single litter in spring, 1-8 (occasionally more), born blind and helpless.
Conservation Not threatened. An important fur-bearer. Locally extinct in some parts of the plains, and near to urban areas.
Similar Species Most likely to be confused with weasels or possibly martens (which are larger).

Wolverine
Gulo gulo

Size TL 2½-3½ft (80cm-1.12m);
T 6½-10in (17-26cm);
WT 13¼-31½lbs (6-14.4kg).

Identification Although a large weasel it is superficially like a small bear; males are generally larger than females. Dark reddish brown above, with a buff-yellow band along sides, meeting at base of the tail. Tail similar to wolf, but with 5 toes.
Range A mostly Arctic species, found across N Canada and Alaska, and extending south in Rockies to California. It also occurs in the Old World.
Habitat Forest and tundra, in south of range exclusively in high mountain habitats.
Food Omnivorous; a powerful predator killing anything it can catch, including moose caught in snow drifts. Can drive bears from carrion, and often follows trappers taking their catches. Does not conceal its food, but marks them with foul-smalling odor. Also eats berries, shoots and other vegetable matter.
Breeding 2-5 young, blind and helpless, born in a den in rock-cleft, among roots, or in dense brush.
Conservation Much persecuted, and its range is now considerably fragmented; it is probably endangered or extinct in many of the southern parts of its range.
Similar Species Not likely to be confused with any other species.

Badger
Taxidea taxus

2 in
(5 cm)

Size TL 22-33in (57.8-84.5cm);
T 4-6in (10-15.7cm);
WT 8-17lbs (3.6-7.71kg,
occasionally up to 11.4kg).

Identification A relatively large carnivore, with a thick-set body and relatively short legs; males are larger than females. Gray or hornish-gray above, with dark legs and characteristic black-and-white face pattern. Generally nocturnal, particularly in areas close to man.
Range Widespread over W USA, east to Great Lakes, south to Mexico and north to SW Canada.
Habitat Variable, but usually open prairies, farmlands, parkland, and sometimes woodland edge, but not normally in forests.

Food Mostly small mammals such as ground squirrels, prairie dogs, gophers, mice and voles, also ground-nesting birds and their eggs, snakes (including rattlesnakes), and invertebrates.
Breeding A single litter born spring, blind and helpless, but well furred. The den is usually in a burrow.
Conservation Not threatened, but persecuted in some areas, because their burrowing may be a hazard to cattle and horses.
Similar Species Not likely to be confused with any other species.

Spotted Skunk
Spilogale putorius

Size TL 13-22in (34.5-56.3cm);
T 2½-8½in (6.8-21.9cm);
WT 1½-4lbs (784g-1.8kg).

Identification A small black skunk, with white stripes or spots on head and sides, and white tail-tip. When alarmed, stands on forepaws and sprays foul-smelling scent up to 13ft (4m).

Range Fairly widespread in E USA, but absent from most of the East Coast States and New England.

Habitat A wide range of open habitats including woodland, farmland, and scrub, often living in deserted woodchuck burrows.

Food Omnivorous, feeding mostly on small mammals, insects, fruit, reptiles, and carrion.

Breeding A single litter of 4-5 young born in early spring, blind and helpless.

Conservation Not threatened; trapped in significant numbers for its pelt (see Striped Skunk).

Related Species Western Spotted Skunk, *S. gracilis*, is extremely similar in general appearance; it is widespread in W USA and south to Mexico. Several other species have been described, but it is probable that all the Spotted Skunks belong to a single rather variable species.

Striped Skunk
Mephitis mephitis

1½ in
(4 cm)

Size TL 20-30in (52-77cm);
T 6½-15in (17-40cm);
WT 4-9¾lbs (1.8-4.5kg, occasionally up to 5.5kg).

Identification Almost too well known to need description. A large black skunk with broad white stripes from the back of the head to rump; males larger than females.

Range Widespread across North America from extreme SE Yukon and S Northwest Territories, south shore of Hudson's Bay and S Quebec, south through most of USA to N Mexico.

Habitat Occurs in a wide range of habitats, including deserts, farmlands, gardens, and woodlands.

Food Omnivorous, feeding mostly on insects and their grubs, eggs and nestlings of ground-nesting birds, small mammals, as well as fruit and other plant matter.

Breeding A single litter born in February or March, of 2-10 (usually 5-7) young, blind and helpless but covered with fine fur, which shows the pattern.

Conservation Not threatened. One of the most common carriers of rabies - but in perspective, still much lower risk of infecting humans than domestic dogs.

Similar Species Only likely to be confused with the Hooded Skunk, which only occurs in S USA and Mexico.

Hooded Skunk
Mephitis macroura

Size TL 22-31in (55.8-79cm);
T 13-15in (33.2-40cm);
WT 2-2½lbs (965g-1.2kg).

Identification A black skunk with narrow white stripes on the back, and long tail; variable and one color phase has the tail and back almost completely white, another black, but numerous intermediates occur. Males are larger than females
Range Widespread in Mexico, extending into W Texas, SW New Mexico and SE Arizona
Habitat Occur in a wide variety of habitats at altitudes of up to 7874ft (2400m), including deserts and poderosa pine, often close to permanent watercourses.
Food Omnivorous, feeding extensively on insects and their grubs, particularly those obtained by digging; but little known.
Breeding Little known; probably 3-5 young, born blind and helpless in early summer.
Conservation Not threatened.
Similar Species Most likely to be confused with the Striped Skunk, which has a shorter tail.

Hog-nosed Skunk
Conepatus mesoleucus

Size TL 20-26in (52.5-67.3cm);
T 7½-11¼in (19-28.6cm); WT 2¼-5¾lbs
(1.1-2.7kg, occasionally 4.5kg).

Identification A large white-backed skunk, unlikely to be
confused with any other species, except Hooded and Striped
Skunks, both of which usually have black tails, or black on the
back. Defends itself with powerful spray of foul scent. Mostly
nocturnal, and can be detected by "plowed" areas where they
have been rooting for grubs.
Range Confined to SW USA and Mexico, occurring as far
north as SE Colorado.
Habitat Found mostly in the foothills, and partly wooded
areas as well as rocky areas; rarely around human habitations.
Food Mostly insects, reptiles, and arachnids, with vegetation,
molluscs and small mammals according to season.
Breeding A single litter in late April or May of 3-4 young,
born blind and helpless, in a den in a rock-cleft.
Conservation Not threatened; may be extending their range.
Related Species Eastern or Gulf Coast Hog-Nosed Skunk,
C. leuconotus, is larger with a narrower white stripe on the
back; it is confined to extreme S Texas, and is probably
conspecific with the Hog-nosed.

River Otter
Lutra canadensis

3 in
(7.5 cm)

Size TL 3-4ft (91.5cm-1.27m);
T 12-19in (30-50cm);
WT 11-30lbs (5-13.7kg).

Identification A long, slender, aquatic carnivore, rarely seen far from water. It is brown above, paler below with a blunt muzzle, fairly short limbs, and a long, tapering tail.
Range Formerly found throughout most of North America; now rare or extinct in many parts of USA.
Habitat Almost all wetlands, from seashores and estuaries, to lakes and ponds, generally with cover, particularly woodlands.
Food A wide range including fish, water birds, small mammals, crustaceans, and amphibians.
Breeding A single litter born in a den among roots, in burrow; 1-6 (usually 2-4) young, born helpless and blind, but fully furred.

Conservation Has undergone dramatic declines, but still widespread and abundant in some areas.
Similar Species Only likely to be confused with Sea Otter (West Coast only), Mink, which are much smaller, or Beaver which are more robust and lack the otter's long tapering tail.

Sea Otter
Enhydra lutris

Size TL 2½-5¾ft (76cm-1.8m);
T 10-14in (26-36cm);
WT 25-59lbs (11.4-27kg, occasionally up to 45kg).

Identification A distinctive coastal marine mammal; a large otter, confined to the oceans where it often swims on its back and very rarely seen ashore. Often seen with cubs.
Range Coastal waters of North America as far south as Monterey, California and north to Aleutian Islands; also USSR coastal waters.

Habitat Exclusively marine, often associated with kelp beds; rarely seen on shore.
Food Shellfish and sea urchins, which it smashes open with a rock on its chest.
Breeding A single (rarely twins) pup born at sea, in all months of the year; fully developed and active within a day, and swimming at 2 weeks.
Conservation Once on the brink of extinction, but now spreading, particularly in California
Similar Species Most likely to be confused with seals, which lack long tail.

Mountain Lion
Felis concolor

3 in
(7.5 cm)

Size TL 5-9ft (1.5-2.7m);
T 20-36in (53-92cm);
WT 75-275lbs (34-125kg).

Identification A large cat, also known as the cougar or puma. It is unlikely to be mistaken for any other species if seen clearly. Buff to tawny above, paler below, with a long slender, black-tipped tail.

Range Formerly most of the Americas; in North America mostly confined to West, with isolated populations in Appalachians and Florida.

Habitat Very varied; from forests to swamps and deserts.

Food Mostly mammals, particularly deer, beaver, porcupines, rabbits, and beaver; also birds and sometimes insects such as grasshoppers and even significant quantities of grass; occasionally domestic livestock, particularly sheep.

Breeding Usually alternate breed years; litter of 1-6 (usually 2-4) blind and helpless at birth. Den in a cave, among rocks, in dense brush.

Conservation Mountain Lion has been extirpated over most of USA, but with increasing protection is recolonising some of its former habitats.

Related Species Jaguar, *F. onca*, is a large spotted cat, which once ranged as far north as Colorado, is now extremely rare, if not extinct, in North America; confined to SW Texas and Mexico.

Ocelot
Felis pardalis

Size 3-4¼ft (92cm-1.3m);
T 10½-15in (27-40cm);
WT 20-35lbs (9.1-15.8kg).

Identification A medium-sized cat, with distinctive, and very attractive, markings, and a long tail. Unlikely to be confused with any other species, except possibly the Jaguar (which is much larger, and invariably has "rosette" markings).
Range Confined to Texas, Arkansas, Louisiana, Arizona and possibly Oklahoma; also through Mexico to South America.
Habitat Wooded and scrub habitats.
Food Mostly birds and small mammals, also reptiles and insects, fish and some domestic animals and poultry.
Breeding Single litter of 2-4 young, blind and helpless.
Conservation Endangered and threatened over most of its range; it has declined as a result of collecting for pet trade and hunting for its pelt, with few recent observations. It is protected and the import of skins and live animals prohibited.
Related Species Feral House Cats, *F. catus*, occur widely and are often surprisingly numerous; they are extremely variable, resembling any of their domestic ancestors, and are frequently augmented by abandoned pets. Jaguarundi, *F. yagaouroundi*, occurs in Mexico and extreme S USA, where it is endangered; it is a small slender cat, gray, black or reddish.

Lynx
Felis lynx

Size TL 2-3½ft (67cm-1m);
T 2-5½in (5-14cm);
WT 10-43¾lbs (4.5-19.9kg).

3 in
(7.5 cm)

Identification Thick soft fur, grayish brown, mixed with buff or pale brown above, grayer below. The short tail has a black tip, and the ears have long, prominent tufts. Males are larger than females.
Range Confined to N North America from Alaska to Newfoundland, and to US border around Great Lakes, and through Rockies to Colorado.
Habitat Almost exclusively deep forest, particularly conifers, also tundra, particularly in "starvation years" (after crashes in cyclical populations of hares, lemmings).
Food Mammals, up to the size of small deer, and birds, particularly Snowshoe Hares.
Breeding Single litter of 1-5 (usually 2 or 3); young born blind and helpless.
Conservation Much reduced over most the southern parts of its range. Since an individual may range over 60-85 sq miles (155-220sq km), large reserves are needed to support a viable population. Hunted for their pelts, particularly in Canada.
Similar Species Most likely to be confused with Bobcat, which is shorter-legged, with smaller ear-tufts, and has the tail black only on upperside.

Bobcat
Felis rufa

1⅞ in
(4.5 cm)

Size TL 22-47in (56.2cm-1.2m);
T 3½-7¾in (9-20.1cm);
WT 8¼-56¾lbs (3.8-25.8kg).

Identification A medium-sized cat, with thick soft fur, which
is yellowish brown or buff above, flecked with black, and
whitish with black spots below. Upper parts of legs banded.
The males are larger than females.

Range Found over most of USA and south into Mexico, also
in S Canada. Absent from much of the Midwest.

Habitat Found in a wide variety of habitats, including scrub,
open woodlands and forest, rocky deserts, and even swamps.

Food Wide range of animals up to the size of deer; also
porcupines, hares, and occasionally domestic stock.

Breeding Single litter of 1-6 (usually 3 or 4) young,
(occasionally second litter in south of range); blind and
helpless; born April-May in a den in a hollow tree or rock cleft.

Conservation Has declined in many areas of human
settlement, but is still abundant in some areas.

Related Species Only likely to be confused with Lynx; the
Bobcat's tail is proportionally longer, with two or three black
bars, and the black on tip is only on upper surface.

Northern Fur Seal
Callorhinus ursinus

Size TL 8ft (up to 2.5m);
WT 496lbs (up to 225kg).

Identification Males blackish above, reddish brown below, with massive, grayish shoulders; females much smaller and grayer. Both sexes have very long flippers, a short, pointed snout and long whiskers.

Range More pelagic than most seals, migrating up to 6200 miles (9978km) to breeding grounds on Pribilofs, Alaska, also San Miguel, California and islands in USSR.

Habitat Marine, coming on shore to breed, and occasionally to rest.

Food Fish (including herring, rockfish, mackerel), squid, and cuttlefish.

Breeding In colonies (rookeries) on islands, where the males gather harems. A single well-furred pup born in summer.

Conservation Ruthlessly exploited from the late 18th century to the beginning of 20th century. The most serious threats are now from man-made debris such as fishing nets, plastic bands, polythene bags and oil spills.

Similar Species Most likely to be confused with Guadalupe Fur Seal, but only in south of range, but latter is rare. Sea lions and elephant seals are larger.

Guadalupe Fur Seal
Arctocephalus townsendi

Size TL 6½ft (up to about 2m);
WT 350lbs (up to 159kg).

Identification The smallest of the sea lions in North American waters, the males are much larger than females. Nearly black, lighter below, particularly on chest. The snout is rather elongated. The flippers are long and often held overlapping when at rest on the surface of the water.
Range Breeding range restricted to Islas Guadalupe, Baja California; formerly bred Channel Islands, California. As numbers continue to increase, will probably recolonise some Californian islands.
Habitat Coastal marine, breeding in caves on rocky islands.
Food Fish, shellfish.
Breeding Breed in small colonies, consisting of bull and harem of females; single pup born in summer.
Conservation Prior to exploitation in the 19th century c.200,000 on Guadalupe, and populations of unknown size on other islands in area. Believed extinct in 1928, but relocated in 1950s with 14 discovered in 1954. Since then has steadily increased with over 1000 by late 1980s. Sightings in Californian waters are becoming increasingly frequent.
Similar Species Other sea lions, all of which are larger, and generally not as dark.

Northern or Steller's Sea Lion
Eumetopias jubatus

Size TL 9¾ft (up to 3m);
WT 1980lbs (up to 900kg).

Identification Buff or brown, or even yellowish. The males
weigh about 3 times as much as females, and have a mass of
coarse fur around the neck. Pups are dark brown or blackish at
birth.
Range Occurs widely in north Pacific, breeding in California
(Ano Nuevo and Channel Islands), and Washington north to
Alaska. It also breeds in west Pacific in Japan and USSR.
Habitat Marine, breeding on islands and coasts.
Food Fish (including salmon, shad and lampreys, which they
seek in rivers), squid. Males have been seen to kill and eat
other seal pups.
Breeding Males (bulls) gather harems of about 20-30 cows,
and a single pup is born in late spring or early summer.
Conservation Once heavily depleted, but under protection
has recovered in many areas and is continuing to increase.
Similar Species Other sea lions, which
are generally smaller.

Californian Sea Lion
Zalophus californianus

Size TL 8ft (up to 2.5m);
WT 660lbs (up to 300kg).

Identification The most familiar sea lion - frequently
exhibited in circuses and aquaria. Even in the wild it often
appears to be playing and performing, and is usually very
vocal, with a characteristic bark. It is brownish or buff, but
when wet appears black. Males are much larger than females.
Range Occurs widely on the Pacific Coast of North America,
from Vancouver south to Baja California, breeding on islands
from Channel Islands, California, south.
Habitat Coastal marine, hauling out on rocky shores and
breeding on islands.
Food Fish, squid, octopus, abalone, rock fish.
Breeding Breeds in colonies, with the bulls (males) gathering
harems of cows. A single, dark furred, active pup born May-June.
Conservation Although its numbers are much reduced, due
to overhunting, under strict protection it is increasing and is
now common along much of the West Coast; it is resident in
San Fransisco Bay. Probably extinct in Japanese waters.
Similar Species Most likely to be confused with Northern
Sea Lion, which is larger and paler, or Guadalupe Fur Seal,
which is smaller.

Walrus
Odobenus rosmarus

Size TL 11¾ft (up to 3.6m);
WT 1½ tons (up to 1.6 tonnes).

Identification A large, sociable seal, with bare pinkish,
reddish or yellowish-brown skin, and characteristic tusks and
bristly muzzle. The males are larger than females, and have
longer tusks (up to 3¼ft (1m)).
Range Has a circumpolar distribution; two populations occur
in the New World, those in the Pacific-Arctic are larger than
those of the Atlantic-Arctic. Occasionally drifts further south.
Habitat Marine, along the edge of pack ice, normally in
waters less than 60ft (18m) deep.
Food Principally mollusks and crustaceans gathered on the
seabed.
Breeding In colonies, often large. The cows bear a single pup
alternate years.
Conservation Although still relatively abundant, it has been
over-exploited and many populations are considerably
reduced. It is now protected throughout its range, except from
Eskimos.
Similar Species No likely confusion with
other species.

Harbor Seal
Phoca vitulina

Size TL 5½ft (up to 1.7m);
WT 220lbs (up to 100kg).

Identification A small seal, with a dog-like head. Its coloring
is variable but generally bluish gray above with dark blotches
and streaks; the underside is silvery with scattered spots.
Range There are 2 main populations: one in East Coast
waters from Carolinas north to Hudson's Bay; the other in
West Coast waters from Baja California, north to Alaska,
Aleutians, and NW Canada. Also several land-locked
populations in British Columbia and Quebec.

Habitat Coastal marine, often swimming up rivers and
estuaries, as its name suggests. Also lakes.
Food Mostly fish, (including herring, smelt, cod, flounder,
and hake), also cephalopods, mollusks, and crustaceans.
Breeding Single (occasionally twins), well-developed pup
born in early summer.
Conservation Widespread, but locally populations have
declined; however under protection they are thriving in most
of their range. The most serious threats are from pollution.
Liable to desert beaches if frequently disturbed.
Related Species Largha or Spotted Seal, *P. largha*, is similar,
but paler; it is confined to ice floes in north Pacific.

Ribbon Seal
Phoca fasciata

Size TL 5¾ft (up to 1.8m);
WT 198lbs (up to 90kg).

Identification A small seal with a characteristic dark brown
or black contrasting with creamy white bands around the neck,
along sides and over rump. Both sexes have similar markings,
and the males are slightly larger than females. Distinctive
pattern distinguishes it from all other seals within its range.
Range Breeds only in the Arctic of Alaska and also Siberia,
occurring as far south as the limit of drifting pack ice. Occurs
as far south as the Alaskan Peninsula.
Habitat Marine, breeding on floating ice.
Food Fish, squid and other cephalopods.
Breeding A single white-coated pup is born March-April.
Conservation Not known to be threatened, and only hunted
in small numbers by Eskimos.
Similar Species Most closely resembles Harp Seal, and is
probably closely related, but their ranges do not overlap.

Ringed Seal
Phoca hispida

Size TL 5¼ft (up to 1.6m);
WT 198lbs (up to 90kg).

Identification The smallest seal, generally dark gray or
grayish black above, light gray below, with a pattern of pale
oval rings on the upperside, hence its name.

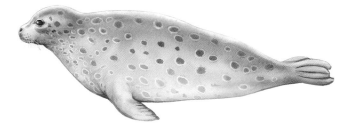

Range Has a circumpolar distribution. In North America
occurs as far south as Labrador and Newfoundland, the south
shore of Hudson's Bay and Point Barrow in Alaska.
Habitat Mostly associated with ice, digging breathing holes
with their flippers.
Food Largely opportunistic, feeding on fish, plankton
crustaceans.
Breeding Single white-coated pup is born in a den excavated
in ice in March-April.
Conservation Not known to be threatened.
Similar Species Most likely to be confused with Harbor
Seal, which lacks the ringed pattern.

Harp Seal
Phoca groenlandica

Size TL 6½ft (up to 2m);
WT 330 lbs (up to 150kg).

Identification Males are creamy white or grayish above with
a blackish, harp-shaped marking on the back; the markings of
the females and juveniles are less distinct and grayer.
Range Found in Arctic waters on both sides of the Atlantic.
In North America from north of Hudson's Bay to Gulf of St
Lawrence.
Habitat Closely associated with drifting pack ice.
Food Mostly fish and crustaceans.
Breeding On ice; a single white-coated pup is
born in February-March.
Conservation Populations considerably reduced by over-
exploitation, but probably not endangered as seal populations
usually show remarkable powers of recovery.
Similar Species Most likely to be confused with Atlantic
Seal, which is grayer, and has distinctive profile.

Bearded Seal
Erignathus barbatus

Size TL 11ft (up to 3.4m);
WT 750lbs (up to 340kg or more).

Identification A large seal, gray or yellowish gray, sometimes brownish on face and neck, with characteristic "beard" of bristles. The bristles end in a tight spiral. The front flippers are also distinctive, having a rather square appearance.
Range Has a circumpolar distribution; in North America occurs as far south as Alaskan Peninsula, south shore of Hudson's Bay and Labrador. Occasionally as far south as Gulf of St Lawrence.
Habitat Mostly found in coastal waters and shallow seas, preferring drifting pack ice.

Food Almost exclusively bottom-dwelling invertebrates and slow-moving fish.
Breeding Generally solitary but sometimes breeds in small, loose colonies; a single brown-coated pup born April-May.
Conservation Not threatened.
Similar Species Not likely to be confused with other seals within range, if seen at close quarters.

Gray or Atlantic Seal
Halichoerus grypus

Size TL 7½ft (up to 2.3m);
WT 680lbs (up to 310kg).

Identification A large grayish to blackish seal, marked with
blotches; paler on the underside. The profile is characteristic.
Range Occurs in northern waters on both sides of the
Atlantic; in New World ranges from Newfoundland south to
Gulf of St Lawrence and coast of New England.
Habitat Coastal waters.
Food Mostly fish, often congregating in estuaries to feed on
salmon. Also pollack, flounders, cod, whiting, and
crustaceans.
Breeding Breeds in small groups with bulls forming
harems; a single white-coated pup is born January-February.

Conservation A rare species, which is persecuted because of
the damage it does to fishing gear.
Related Species Most likely to be confused with the Bearded
Seal, which has a prominent beard, or the Harbor Seal, which
is smaller with a domed head.

Hooded Seal
Cystophora cristata

Size TL 8ft (up to 2.5m);
WT 880lbs (up to 400kg).

Identification A grayish seal with brownish and cream
blotches, and paler on the underside; the markings of the
females are less distinct than males. Both sexes have a
characteristic inflatable nasal sac on the top of the head (larger
in the males).
Range Occurs in Arctic waters on both sides of Atlantic. In
North America ranges from Baffin Island south to Gulf of St
Lawrence, but absent from Hudson's Bay.
Habitat Found mostly in deep waters close to pack ice.
Food Fish and cephalopods, including capelin, halibut,
redfish, cod, squid and amphipods.

Breeding Monogamous; the single blue-gray pup is born on
ice, in the second half of March.
Conservation Has been heavily hunted, and although
probably depleted in many areas is not endangered.
Similar Species Not likely to be confused with other seals.

Northern Elephant Seal
Mirounga angustirostris

Size TL males 21ft (6m), females 11ft (3.5m).

Identification A huge seal. Brown or grayish above, paler below. The adult male (bull) has a large trunk-like snout, which is inflated during the breeding season.

Range Confined to coastal waters along Pacific coast from Gulf of Alaska to Baja California. It breeds on Farallon Islands of California and other islands south to San Benito of Baja California.

Habitat Because of their size they are more or less restricted to breeding on sandy beaches.

Food Fish, including sharks, squid and other deepwater marine life.

Breeding Bulls arrive on breeding grounds in December, and establish territories for their harems. The black-furred pups are born in December-January, but do not finally take to sea until May.

Conservation From an all-time low of about 20 animals in 1911, have recovered and continue to increase and spread. After reaching 70,000 in the 1980s their increase is slowing.

Similar Species Only likely to be confused with other seals, which are much smaller. Whales and sharks and large fish are much more streamlined, mostly with a dorsal fin.

Manatee
Trichechus manatus

Size TL 15ft (up to 4.6m);
WT 1925lbs (875kg).

Identification A large, dark, grayish, streamlined, aquatic
mammal, with a broad, flattened tail, and paddle-like flippers;
the upper lip is covered in stiff bristles. Normally only the
foreparts are seen out of the water, but since they often occur
in clear shallow waters and can be spotted from the air.
Range Caribbean as far north as Florida and Carolinas.
Populations are now fragmented and the only substantial
populations are in Florida.
Habitat Confined to warm, coastal waters, estuaries, rivers and
inlets. They cannot survive a temperature of below 46°F (8°C).
Food Entirely herbivorous, grazing on aquatic vegetation.
Breeding Have a single young every 2 or 3 years, born in the
water. The mother clasps her young to her breast with her
flippers.
Conservation Their numbers are seriously depleted and a
major cause of mortality has been injury from power-boat
propellors. Manatees are slow moving, and cannot dive fast
enough to avoid injury
Similar Species None in region. Other aquatic mammals,
such as cetaceans are
all more agile.

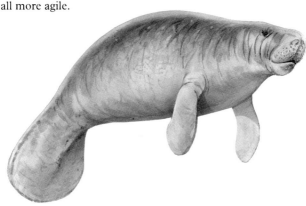

Collared Peccary
Dicotyles (=Pecari) tajacu

1½ in
(4 cm)

Size TL 2¾-3ft (86-96cm);
T ½-2in (1.5-5.5cm);
SH 19-23in (50-60cm); WT 28½-59lbs (13-27kg).

Identification A pig-like mammal, with coarse fur, grizzled grayish or blackish, with a pale collar, and a distinct crest from crown to rump. Usually in small groups.
Range Confined to S Arizona, S Texas and extreme S New Mexico. Also Mexico and south to South America
Habitat Deserts, chaparral, scrub oak, rocky canyons, and often in dense prickly pear thickets.
Food Mostly herbivorous, eating cacti, particularly prickly pear, and other succulent vegetation.
Breeding 1-5 (usually 2) young throughout the year; young are well developed and follow the mother after a few days.
Conservation Formerly much more widespread, occurring north to Arkansas, but hunted for meat and skins. Now protected and hunted as game.
Related Species Wild Boar or Hog, *Sus scrofa*, is the ancestor of the domestic pig, and has been introduced into the USA; escaped hogs have formed feral populations. Wild Boar occur widely in Appalachians, and Feral Hogs occur in California, much of S USA and Mexico. They are similar to domestic hogs, but with coarse, often thick, usually dark hair.

Mustang or Wild Horse
Equus caballus

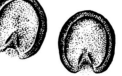

6 in
(15 cm)

Size TL 6½-7¾ft (2-2.4m);
T 19in (50cm);
SH 4¼-4½ft (1.3-1.4m);
WT 594-858lbs (270-390kg).

Identification Too familiar to need detailed description; very variable, but essentially the same as domestic ponies and horses. Distinguished from Burros by long mane and tail.
Range Occurs mostly in western states of USA.
Habitat Almost exclusively found in open grasslands and prairies.
Food Grasses and forbs, also saltbrush, sagebrush and other shrubby plants.
Breeding Stallions (males) gather harems of 5 or 6 females, and there is usually a single foal, in alternate years in poor rangelands.
Conservation Protection introduced in 1971; by 1976 population estimated at over 50,000 and growing rapidly. Their protection is a highly charged and politically sensitive matter.
Related Species Burro, or Feral Ass, *E. asinus*, is usually grayer with a dark cross on its shoulders; it generally occurs in more arid environments than the wild horse.

Elk
Cervus elaphus (=canadensis)

4 in
(10 cm)

Size TL 6½-9½ft (2-2.9m); T 2¼-6½in (6-17cm);
SH up to 4¾ft (1.5m); WT 1100lbs (up to 500kg).

Identification A large reddish-brown deer, with yellowish
rump and tail. Males are larger than females, with shaggy neck
and carry large, branching antlers. During the rut males have a
"bugle" call.

Range Formerly most of North America, now confined to
Rockies, extinct or fragmented in East and in prairies.

Habitat Now mostly found in mountainous habitats,
particularly forests.

Food Variable, depending on habitat; includes grasses,
shrubs, and forbs.

Breeding The males (bulls) defend harems of up to 60 cows
in the fall; a single spotted calf (occasionally twins) is born in
May or June. Active from birth, joining the herd at about a
week old.

Similar Species Most deer are smaller and paler; moose is
larger and more long-legged.

Conservation From a low in 1930s, most populations have
been growing under protection and
management.

Related Species Sika Deer,
C. nippon, has been introduced
from Far East and is fairly
widespread in Texas; scattered
populations exist in Kansas, Oklahoma,
Maryland, Wisconsin, Virginia;
medium-sized, the
males have
antlers similar
to elk.

Mule Deer
Odocoileus hemionus

3¼ in
(8 cm)

Size TL 33½-3¾t ft (1.1-2m);
T 4½-9in (11-23cm);
SH 3¼ft (up to 1m); WT 69¼-473lbs (31.5-215kg).

Identification A medium-sized deer, but variable in size; males always larger than females. Reddish brown or yellowish brown above, underside and inside of legs white; grayer in winter. The ears are large and mule-like, rump white and relatively long tail often black-tipped.
Range Confined to W North America, from S Yukon and Mackenzie south to W Texas and Mexico.
Habitat Variable, including prairies, forest edges, mountains and pastures. Often nocturnal, or active morning and evening.
Food In summer mainly forbs, herbs and grasses, in winter mostly browses on shrubs, saplings, acorns, fungi, and lichens.
Breeding Males attract a harem of females in fall. Young, usually twins or triplets, but only one in young females, are born early summer; the young are heavily spotted.
Conservation Declined over most of its range, with lows in early 20th century. From 1920s increased, recolonizing much of its former range. Now subject to regulated hunts.
Similar Species Most likely to be confused with White-tailed Deer, which has smaller ears and lacks a black tail-tip.

White-tailed Deer
Odocoileus virginianus

3 in
(7.5 cm)

Size TL 4¼-6½t ft (1.3-2m);
T 5¼-13in (15-33cm);
SH 3¼ft (1m); WT 50-300lbs (22-135kg).

Identification Very variable in size. Reddish or yellowish brown above, grayer in winter, and white on underside and inside of legs. The long bushy tail is brownish with white edges, often with a dark stripe down the middle; when alarmed it is held erect. The male has antlers with both beams branching.

Range Widespread over much of North America, north to S Canada, but absent from Far West. Also extends through Mexico to South America.

Habitat Very variable; includes woodlands, pastures, gardens, and farmlands.

Food Browses and grazes on a wide range of grasses, shrubs, trees, and other vegetation.

Breeding Less polygamous than other deer, with some bucks (males) only mating with one doe; rut is in fall, and young (1-3) born in early spring; fawn is heavily spotted at birth and active soon after birth, following the mother within a few days.

Conservation Like other deer, populations were generally at a low ebb earlier this century.

Related Species Fallow Deer, *Cervus dama*, has been introduced, and survive in at least 8 US states, and James Island, British Columbia. It usually spotted in summer.

is

Moose
Alces alces

5¼ in (13 cm)

Size TL 6½-9ft (2-2.8m);
T 6½in (17cm);
SH 6½-7¼ft (2-2.25m);
WT 1210lbs (usually up to 550kg).

Identification The largest deer in the world; dark, long-legged, with a humped appearance and a large muzzle. The males are much larger than females and carry huge (up to 6½ft (2m) across), palmate antlers. Male has loud bellowing call, females a more cow-like "moaning" call.
Range Across most of N North America from New England to Alaska, and south through Rockies to Colorado and Utah. Is migratory in many areas.
Habitat Forests and willow thickets; generally rather aquatic.
Food Mostly browse and aquatic vegetation, particularly willows, aspen and birch.
Breeding Do not form harems; breed in groups ranging in size from a pair to 30 or more. 1-3 calves born in spring; active soon after birth, and follows the mother, and is swimming at about 2 weeks.
Conservation Not threatened; managed as a quarry species.
Similar Species Not likely to be confused with any other deer.

Caribou or Reindeer
Rangifer tarundus

Size TL 4¼-6¾ft (1.3-2.1m);
T 3¾-7¾in (10-20cm);
SH 3¾-3¼ft (90cm-1.05m);
WT 594lbs (up to 270kg).

4 in
(10 cm)

Identification A large deer, variable in color, but usually with shaggy brownish fur, paler on neck, with the underparts and rump whitish. The feet are large and both sexes carry antlers, those of females are smaller than males. Usually encountered in herds of 200 to 100,000.

Range Widespread across far northern North America from Alaska to Newfoundland and south to Rockies in NE Washington, and N Idaho. Among the most migratory of all mammals, following traditional routes.

Habitat Includes tundra, boreal forests, taiga, and mountain coniferous forests.

Food Variable, depending on habitat; includes lichens. They also feed on twigs (willows, birches), sedges, and fungi.

Breeding Breed in large herd, with bull gathering harems of 12-15 cows. Young (1, occasionally 2) are born in May-July, and keep up with the herd within a day of their birth.

Conservation Extinct over southern parts of its former range, which once extended to N New England.

Similar Species Not likely to be confused with other species.

Pronghorn or Antelope
Antilocapra americana

2³/₄ in (7 cm)

Size TL 4-4³/₄in (1.25-1.45m);
T 2¹/₄-6¹/₂in (6-17cm);
SH 2³/₄-3¹/₄ft (86cm-1.03m);
WT 154lbs (up to 70kg).

Identification Sandy brown above, with white belly, chest, and white bands on neck, throat and chin and a large white rump patch; rump hairs can be erected, enlarging it, when alarmed. Both sexes carry short, stout horns; the females' smaller than males'. Fastest land animal in North America.

Range Widespread in W North America, from S Canada to N Mexico. In some areas migratory.

Habitat Open grasslands, shrublands, prairies and deserts.

Food Wide range of vegetation, including forbs, grasses, shrubs and also sometimes grazes on crops including alfalfa and wheat.

Breeding Polygamous; males gather harems of about 20 does. Young, 1-3, are born May-June, and are hidden separately by mother, until they join the herd at a week old.

Conservation At one time believed to have fallen to as few as 20,000, but by late 1970s around 500,000.

Similar Species Not likely to be confused with any other species; no deer have so much white on the rump.

Related Species Indian Blackbuck, *Antilope cervicapra*, has been introduced in Texas.

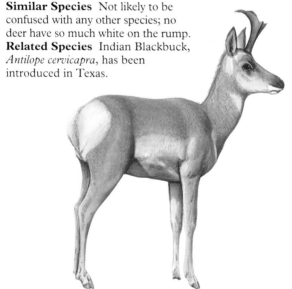

Bison
Bison bison

5 in
(12.5 cm)

Size TL 6¾-12¼ft (2.1-3.8m);
T 17-23in (43-60cm);
SH 5¼-9ft (1.6-2.8m);
WT 0.35 tons (360kg-1.35tonne).

Identification Unmistakable; large, with dark brown, shaggy fur, and curving horns. Usually seen in herds.
Range Confined to refuges, National Parks and private ranches, mostly in western North America, including Wood Buffalo N P, Northwest Territory and Yellowstone N P, Wyoming.
Habitat Variable, including woodlands, forests and prairies
Food Mostly grazers, but also browse, eating a wide range of grasses, sedges, forbs, and shrubs.
Breeding A single calf (occasionally twins) born in May; it follows the herd within a few hours of birth.
Conservation Once an almost incredibly abundant mammal, but within less than half a century almost wiped out. Protected at the last minute, and in the past century has been re-established in many refuges and parks.
Similar Species None in North America.

Mountain Goat
Oreamnos americanus

3¹/₂ in
(9 cm)

Size TL 4-5¾ft (1.2-1.8m);
T 3¼-8in (8-20cm);
SH 3-3½ft (90cm-1m);
WT 300lbs (up to 136kg).

Identification Almost unmistakable with shaggy white or yellowish-white fur and black eyes, nose, horns, and hooves.
Range Confined to Rockies from extreme SE Alaska and Yukon south to W Montana and N Idaho. Introduced extensively in other parts of Rockies, including Nevada, Utah, Wyoming, South Dakota, Colorado, Oregon.
Habitat Restricted to high altitudes, normally in rocky habitats above the timberline. Introductions have been made at lower elevations.
Food Wide range of vegetation including grasses, sedges, forbs, and deciduous shrubs.
Breeding A single fully developed kid born in May-June, active soon after birth.
Conservation A comparatively rare species within most of its range, but not threatened.
Related Species Feral Goat, *Capra hircus*, which is extremely variable in appearance, usually resembling the longer-haired domestic goats, occurs in small numbers in at least 25 US states, and in Canada and Mexico.

Musk Ox
Ovibos moschatus

5 in
(12.5 cm)

Size TL 6¼-8ft (1.9-2.5m);
T 2¼-6¾in (6-17cm);
WT 370-900lbs (167-400kg).

Identification Unmistakable; large with long dark hair, reaching almost to ground. Both sexes have massive horns. Lives in groups of up to c.100. When threatened, form a defensive ring with calves in center.
Range Confined to extreme N Arctic Canada, as far north as Ellesmere Island, and as far south as SW shore of Hudson's Bay. Reintroduced into Alaska, Greenland, and Scandinavia.
Habitat Arctic tundra above the treeline. In winter tends to be found on windswept hilltops where snow is blown away.
Food Lichens, sedges, twigs, shoots, and grasses.
Breeding Single calf born alternate years in April-May; it is active within hours of birth.
Conservation Extirpated from Alaska in 1850-1860, and in 1935 introduced into Nunivak Island from Greenland; reintroduced from Nunivak to mainland Alaska where by 1978 there were about 1000.
Similar Species None.

Bighorn Sheep
Ovis canadensis

3½ in
(9 cm)

Size TL 4¾-6ft (1.5-1.85m); T 3¾-5¾in (10-15cm);
SH 2¾-3¼ft (90cm-1.05m); WT 308lbs (up to 140kg).

Identification A stocky sheep, generally brown above, but
very pale in desert areas, with pale underparts and rump;
males (which are larger than females) have massive spiral
horns; ewes have smaller horns. They are gregarious, living in
herds of up to 100. During rut males can be heard horn
clashing for a mile or more.
Range Confined to W North America from British Columbia
and Alberta south to Mexico.
Habitat Alpine meadows, pastures, prairies, deserts, and
rocky foothills.
Food Wide range of vegetation, particularly grasses and sedges,
and in arid areas browses on bushes, shrubs and even cacti.
Breeding A single (occasionally twins) lamb born in spring in
north, at almost any time of the year in south. It is active soon
after birth.
Conservation Although most surviving populations are not
threatened, at one time many populations were severely
reduced.
Similar Species Dall's Sheep, which is not normally brown,
and occurs further north.

Dall's or Thinborn Sheep
Ovis dalli

3 in
(7.5 cm)

Size TL 3½-5ft (1-1.5m);
T 3-4½in (7.5-11.5cm); SH 2½-3½ft (75cm-1m);
WT 100-200lbs (45-90kg).

Identification A stocky sheep similar to the Bighorn, generally whitish, but in southern part of range a blackish or grayish-brown form occurs (Stone Sheep). Horns of the male are massive, but thinner than Bighorn's.
Range Confined to Alaska and W Canada (British Columbia, Yukon and Northwest Territories).
Habitat Rocky mountainous terrain.
Food Mostly grasses and sedges, but also other vegetation including shrubs.
Breeding Usually a single lamb (occasionally twins), born in early summer, active within hours of birth.
Conservation Not threatened; subject to regulated hunting in many areas.
Similar Species Bighorn Sheep, which occurs further south and is browner.

Barbary Sheep or Aouadad
Ammotragus lervia

Size TL 4¼-6ft (1.3-1.9m); T 9¾in (25cm); SH 2¾-3¼ft (90cm-1.05m); WT 253lbs (up to 115kg).

Identification A smooth-coated, tawny-brown sheep, with a characteristic long beard and goat-like horns, which bend outward.
Range An Old World species, originally from North Africa, introduced widely in SW USA and Mexico.
Habitat Dry canyons, rocky hillsides.
Food Grasses, forbs and shrubs, also crops; they can survive without water, utilizing dew and moisture within vegetation.
Breeding 1-3 lambs born most times of the year, but particularly February-April; the young are active within hours of birth.
Conservation Possibly more abundant in North America, than in its native Africa where it is endangered. May affect native Mule Deer and Bighorns adversely.
Related Species Mouflon, *Ovis musimon*, is an ancestor of the domestic sheep, introduced from Europe to USA but probably only flourishing in Texas. Feral Sheep, *O. aries*, reported sporadically in USA.

Fin Whale
Balaenoptera physalus

Size TL 78ft (up to 24m); WT 77 tons (up to 70 tonnes).

Identification One of the most frequently seen rorqual whales. Rorquals are distinguished from other whales by their long, torpedo-like shape, generally dark bluish-gray coloring, and small fins, set well back, which is clearly visible. Behind the fin the back is distinctly ridged. They are generally fast swimming, and surface exposing the head and blowhole first, then blowing, with a single, tall spout, before diving. Unlike Blue and Sei Whales, Fins occasionally breach.

Fin Whale

Range In spring migrates from subtropical waters to northern waters for summer, often passing close to land, and in fall return south. Some populations are resident.
Habitat Marine.
Food Fish and plankton, which is filtered by skimming, usually close to the surface.
Breeding Births occur most months of the year, and a single calf is born, every second or third year.
Conservation All rorquals are depleted, but protected in most parts of the world.
Related Species Blue Whale, *B. musculus*, is the largest living animal, now very rare, but occasionally seen off Atlantic

Blue Whale

and Pacific coasts of North America; it is similar to Fin, but has a broader snout with a distinctive ridge from blowhole to snout. Sei Whale, *B. borealis*, grows to about 59ft (18m) is found in both Atlantic and Pacific waters. It can be distinguished from other rorquals by having its fin further forward. Bryde's Whale, *B. edeni*, is almost indistinguishable from the Sei in the field; it only occurs in warmer waters. **Minke Whale,** *B. acutorostrata*, is the smallest of the rorquals, usually less than 30ft (9m), and often has a white band on the flippers. It is the most abundant rorqual and often the most frequently encountered.

Minke Whale

Humpback Whale
Megaptera novaeangliae

Size TL 40ft (up to 12.4m); WT 52 tons (up to 48 tonnes).

Identification A large relatively slow-moving whale, with exceptionally long, often white, flippers, and a clearly visible fin. When it blows its spout is short and bushy. Humpbacks are extremely acrobatic, frequently breach, and as they dive often throw their tail fluke in the air. They also slap the water with their flippers or tail.

Range Widely distributed in all oceans, and are frequently seen on migration along coasts of North America, particularly California, New England and E Canada, often concentrating in shallow coastal waters.
Habitat Marine.
Food Fish and plankton.
Breeding A single calf is born alternate years.
Conservation Like all other whales, depleted, but possibly increasing under protection, and in New England and Canadian waters has been described as locally common. Often entangled in fishing gear.
Similar Species Only likely to be confused with other large whales at a distance.

Gray Whale
Eschrichtius gibbosus

Size TL 46ft (up to 14.1m); WT 38 tons (up to 35 tonnes).

Identification A relatively large whale with a narrow head, and only bumps or ridges on the back - no dorsal fin. It is mottled gray, and often has barnacles and "whale lice." When it blows it produces a single spout. Acrobatic, breaching and "spy-hopping."

Range From May - November in northern Pacific and Arctic waters, the rest of the year migrating to and from, and in, the breeding waters around Baja California.

Habitat Marine, often in shallow coastal waters.

Food Mostly bottom-living crustaceans.

Breeding The single calf (every 2 or more years) is born in January - March.

Conservation Once severely depleted by overhunting; following protection in 1946, the populations migrating along the west coast of North America have increased to over 15,000 and are now the center of a significant tourist industry.

Similar Species The only other large whales without a dorsal fin are the Right Whales, which are black, and the Sperm Whales, which are a different shape.

Right Whale
Balaena glacialis

Size TL 55ft (up to 17m); WT 110 tons (up to 100 tonnes).

Identification A large whale lacking a dorsal fin, and with large head and stongly arched jaws. Often white patches and callosities ("bonnet") on head. The "blow" is distinctive: two spouts producing a "V" shape.

Range Occurs off Atlantic coast of E Canada, as far north as Newfoundland, and south to Florida and Gulf of Mexico. The Pacific population occurs from Bering Sea and Gulf of Alaska south to Baja California.

Habitat Marine.

Food Plankton.

Breeding A single young every 3 or 4 years.

Conservation Called the "right" whale, because it was the right whale to kill. It was slow moving and did not sink when dead. Earlier this century it was still possible to see herds of 100, but now groups of 2-12 are more likely. Although most populations have been protected since 1937, their recovery has been slow in most areas.

Similar Species Bowhead, *B. mystacinus*, is very similar, but lacks the distinctive white "bonnet" of Northern Right Whale; it is one of the rarest whales in the world, but can be seen in Alaskan waters, where it is still hunted.

Northern Bottle-nosed Whale
Hyperoodon ampullatus

Size TL 32ft (up to 10m); WT 4 tons (up to 3.6 tonnes), occasionally more.

Identification A large beaked whale with characteristic head profile. It has a dorsal fin and its blow is a strong globular cloud of spray. Usually in groups of 4-10. Often tame, approaching boats.
Range Confined to northern Atlantic.
Habitat Marine.
Food Mostly squid, but also fish including herrings.
Breeding Single calf born in April or May.

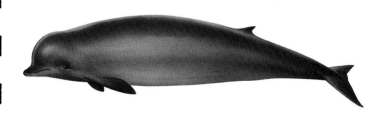

Conservation Easy to hunt and it is probably more depleted than other whales. It comes to the assistance of injured whales in its group, making it even easier to slaughter whole pods.
Related Species Northern Bottle-nosed Whale is one of the most frequently encountered beaked whales in the family Ziphiidae. Others occurring in North American waters are Baird's Beaked Whale, *Berardius bairdii*, which is found in the Pacific; Goose-beaked or Cuvier's Whale, *Ziphius cavirostris*, which occurs in both Pacific and Atlantic waters; True's Beaked Whale, *Mesoplodon mirus*, Sowerby's Beaked Whale, *M. bidens*, and Gervais' Beaked Whale, *M. europaeus*, which are found in Atlantic waters; Gingo-toothed Whale, *M. ginkgodens*, Stejneger's Beaked Whale, *M. steijnegeri*, and Dense Beaked Whale, *M. densirostris*, are found in Pacific. They are all relatively difficult to identify in the field.

Sperm Whale
Physeter catodon

Size TL 49ft (up to 15m); WT 40 tons (36 tonnes), formerly much larger.

Identification The largest of the toothed whales with males larger than females; quite unmistakable. It has a massive head, with a narrow jaw, and is usually grayish, often quite pale; it lacks a dorsal fin, but has a series of bumps. Its blowhole is on the tip of its head and its blow produces a pointing forwards spout; it may blow up to 20 times before diving. It usually lives in groups of up to 20-30.

Range Occurs in all oceans, mostly in deep waters.

Habitat Marine.

Food Almost entirely squid, feeding at depths of up to ½ mile (1km) or more.

Breeding In warm tropical waters. Usually a single calf (rarely twins) about every 4 years.

Conservation Depleted, but still widespread.

Related Species Pygmy Sperm Whale, *Kogia breviceps*, and Dwarf Sperm Whale, *K. simus*, are little-known species growing to about 1½ft (3.5m). They are superficially like a small sperm whale, but lack the greatly enlarged head, and have a dorsal fin.

Harbor or Common Porpoise
Phocoena phocoena

Size TL 5¾ft (up to 1.8m); WT 198lbs (up to 90kg).

Identification A small, rather stout species, dark gray or black above, white below, with a small triangular dorsal fin. Usually seen in small groups (10-15). Often swim near the surface "porpoising."
Range Widespread in Atlantic, Pacific and Arctic waters, as far south as Baja California and Carolinas.
Habitat Usually in shallow coastal waters, estuaries, harbours; often travels up rivers.
Food Fish, including herring; also crustaceans and squid.
Breeding A single young born in early spring, alternate years.
Conservation Numbers much reduced over most its range; significant numbers drown in gill nets and trawls, and small numbers are hunted by Eskimos.

Related Species Gulf Porpoise, *P. sinus*, was recognized as a distinct species as recently as 1950, in the Gulf of California, where it is the only porpoise to occur. Dall's Porpoise, *Phocoenoides dalli*, is a distinctive black-and-white porpoise; it is mostly black with a contrasting white belly, white rear to the dorsal fin and white edges to the tail flukes; it occurs off west coast, from California to Alaska.

Short-finned Pilot Whale
Globiocephala sieboldii (=macrorhynchus)

Size TL 22ft (up to 6.75m); WT 3¼ tons (up to 3 tonnes).

Identification A medium-sized cetacean, with a rounded forehead - the "melon". Blackish with relatively long, narrow flippers. Often in large groups (pods) - up to 200.
Range Widespread in Atlantic waters, as far north as New England, and also Pacific waters from Baja California to Alaskan Peninsula.
Habitat Marine.
Food Mostly squid, apparently feeding mainly at night.
Breeding A single calf every 3 years.
Conservation Although they have been extensively hunted they are still widespread and reasonably abundant.
Related Species Long-finned Pilot Whale, *G. melaena*, is very similar, but with longer, narrower flippers. It is found in Atlantic waters of North America, and may have occurred in north Pacific prior to about 1000 AD.

Killer Whale
Orca orcinus

Size TL 31ft (up to 9.75m); WT 8 tons (up to 7.2 tonnes).

Identification A very distinctive medium-sized cetacean, black and white with a very tall, shark-like, triangular dorsal fin (up to 6ft (2m) high). They often travel in pods of 5-25.
Range Occur in all oceans.
Habitat Marine.

Food Carnivorous, preying on cetaceans including young rorquals and other great whales, hunting in packs; seals, sea lions, sea birds, squid, and other fish.
Breeding A single calf every 2 or 3 years.
Conservation Somewhat persecuted because alleged competition with human fisheries, but not threatened over most of its range.
Related Species False Killer Whale, *Pseudorca crassidens*, is superficially similar to uniformly dark Killer Whales, and difficult to distinguish at a distance. At close range they can be seen to lack the white patches and will ride the bow wave of slower ships. It occurs in Pacific and Atlantic waters off North America. Pygmy Killer Whale, *Feresa attenuata*, is a very little-known species, which occurs in the Atlantic and Pacific Oceans, and may occasionally occur in coastal waters.

Common Dolphin
Delphinus delphis

Size TL 8ft (up to 2.5m); WT 180lbs (up to 82kg).

Identification A small dolphin, with a large beak; it is black on most of the back, with a variable amount of gray on the tail, white on the underside and buff-yellow along the sides. They are extremely gregarious, often forming schools of 1000+ and over 100,000 have been recorded feeding on concentrations of fish. They frequently ride bow waves.

Range In North America, occurs in Pacific waters as far north as S Canada, and in the Atlantic as far north as Nova Scotia and Labrador.

Habitat Marine, mostly in deeper waters, but occasionally coming close to shore and even into rivers.

Food Fish, including flying fish.

Breeding A single young every 2 or 3 years.

Conservation Has been hunted extensively throughout human history. More recently large numbers killed in drift nets, nets set for tuna, and trawls.

Similar Species Most likely to be confused with *Lagenorhynchus* dolphins.

Grampus or Risso's Dolphin
Grampus griseus

Size TL 13ft (up to 4m); WT 1496lbs (up to 680kg).

Identification In general appearance rather similar to pilot whales, but grayer with shorter flippers. The fin is tall and the body is usually extensively scarred. They usually live in groups of 25 upwards to several hundred, and often associate with other cetaceans, particularly pilot whales.
Range Worldwide in temperate and tropical waters.
Habitat Marine, mostly in deep waters.
Food Squid, and some fish.
Breeding Little-known; probably a single young every 2 or 3 years.
Conservation Not known to be threatened.
Similar Species Most likely to be confused with pilot whales.

Pacific White-sided Dolphin
Lagenorhynchus obliquidens

Size TL 7¾ft (up to 2.4m); WT 308lbs (up to 140kg).

Identification A small dolphin with a short, rounded snout. It has a distinctive pattern, with black-and-white markings on a dark gray background. They are fast, often swimming with the sharply hooked dorsal fin, which is dark on the front edge, pale at the rear, cutting through the water's surface. Often in schools of 1000+, often mixed with other sea mammals such as seals and sea lions, and they often ride bow waves.

Range Confined to north Pacific; in North American waters found from Alaska to Baja California.

Habitat Marine.

Food Fish and squid, feeding mostly at night.

Breeding Single young born in late summer or fall.

Conservation Not threatened but some are drowned in gill nets and drift nets.

Related Species Atlantic White-sided Dolphin, *L. acutus*, and White-beaked Dolphin, *L. albirostris* are confined to colder waters of N Atlantic, occurring off eastern seaboard of North America as far south as New England. Pacific White-sided Dolphins have a very similar range to Right-whale Dolphins, *Lissodelphis borealis*, and often form mixed schools. The latter is long and slender, black above, white below, and lacks a dorsal fin.

Spotted and Spinner Dolphins
Stenella spp

Size TL 11¼ft (up to 3.5m); WT 363lbs (up to 165kg).

Identification Among the most difficult of the dolphins to identify in the field. They all have a prominent beak, and are generally gray above, paler below sometimes with spotting or striping. They usually travel in groups of 5-30, which coalesce to form schools of several thousand. They also often associate with tuna fish.

Range Striped Dolphin, *S. coeruleoalba*, and **Spotted Dolphin,** *S. attenuata*, are both found in warmer waters of Atlantic and Pacific; **Atlantic Spotted Dolphin,** *S. plagiodon*, is confined to Atlantic; Tropical Spinner Dolphin, *S. longirostris*, lacks spots or stripes and is found in warmer waters of Pacific and Atlantic; Atlantic Spinner, *S. clymene*, has a distinctive head pattern, and is confined to warm waters of Atlantic.

Habitat Marine.

Food Fish and squid.

Breeding A single young born every 2 or 3 years.

Conservation These are the dolphins most seriously threatened by purse-seine netting for tuna fish. Thousands have been drowned in fishing gear.

Atlantic Spotted Dolphin

Spotted Dolphin

Bottle-nosed Dolphin
Tursiops truncatus

Size TL 13ft (up to 4m); WT 440lbs (up to 200kg, occasionally 650kg).

Identification The familiar dolphin most frequently exhibited in dolphinaria and aquaria. A relatively large dolphin, bluish-gray above, paler below with a prominent beak. Usually in small groups, which may form schools of several thousand. Often ride bow waves of boats.
Range Widespread in Atlantic and Pacific waters.
Habitat Marine, often in coastal lagoons and bays, sometimes ascending rivers.
Food Fish, mostly bottom-dwelling.
Breeding A single young is born every 2 years.
Conservation Has been extensively hunted, and many killed in other fisheries. Probably less numerous than formerly over much of its range, but little data.

Related Species The population occurring in Pacific waters of North America is sometimes treated as a full species - *T. gilli.*

White Whale or Beluga
Delphinapterus leucas

Size TL 15ft (up to 4.6m); WT 1½ tons (up to 1.5 tonnes).

Identification Unmistakable when adult - pure, milky white; young are pinkish brown at birth, becoming dark gray then white at maturity. Usually gregarious, sometimes gathering in groups of several thousand.

White Whale

Range Confined to the colder, Arctic waters of Canada and Alaska; some populations are more or less sedentary, others migrate.

Habitat Marine; often in deep water and close to pack ice.

Food Fish (including capelin, cod, char, and sandeels) crustaceans, mostly feeding along the sea bed.

Breeding A single calf every 3 or 4 years.

Conservation Has been heavily exploited, and although commercial hunting has ceased, is still hunted by Eskimos and other native hunters.

Related Species Narwhal, *Monodon monoceros*, shares the range of the Beluga; it is slightly larger than the Beluga, heavily dappled with dark gray above, and the males carry a single, long (up to 10ft (3m)) tusk.

Narwhal

Further Reading

AMERICAN SOCIETY OF MAMMALOGISTS
A specialist organisation publishing mostly technical works, including Mammalian Species, a series of loose-leaf articles on selected species.

Chapman, Joseph A. and Feldhamer, George A., *Wild Mammals of North America*. 1982. John Hopkins University Press. An excellent source of technical information on the life histories of mammals.

Gelder, Richard G. van, *Mammals of the National Parks*. 1982. John Hopkins University Press. A very useful guide for beginners.

Hall, Raymond E., *The Mammals of North America*. 2 vols. 1981. John Wiley & Sons. A comprehensive handbook - not for the beginner.

Leatherwood, S and Reeves, R. R., *The Sierra Club Handbook of Whales and Dolphins*. 1983. Comprehensive and well illustrated.

MacClintock, Dorcas, *Squirrels of North America*. 1970. Van Nostrand Reinhold Co. A readable account dealing with all species.

Matthiessen, Peter, *Wildlife in America*. 1959, revised 1987. Viking. A highly readable account; includes much about America's threatened mammals.

Murrie, O., *Animal Tracks*. 2nd edn. 1974. Houghton Mifflin Co.

Stokes, Donald and Lilian, *Animal Tracking and Behavior*. 1986. Little, Brown & Company. A useful guide which really helps find mammals.

Tuttle, Merlin D., *America's Neighborhood Bats*. 1988. University of Texas Press. A good introduction with a conservation bias.

Whitaker, John O. Jr, *The Audubon Society Guide to North American Mammals*. 1980 Knopf. A photographic guide with comprehensive coverage.

Index

Note: Page references in bold type indicate full range of data